House of Commons, J. Hamilton Gray

Extracts From the Hon. J.H. Gray's Preliminary Report on the Statutory Laws

Ontario, New Brunswick, and Nova Scotia. Presented to the House of Commons

House of Commons, J. Hamilton Gray

Extracts From the Hon. J.H. Gray's Preliminary Report on the Statutory Laws
Ontario, New Brunswick, and Nova Scotia. Presented to the House of Commons

ISBN/EAN: 9783337154639

Printed in Europe, USA, Canada, Australia, Japan

Cover: Foto ©Suzi / pixelio.de

More available books at **www.hansebooks.com**

EXTRACTS

FROM

THE HON. J. H. GRAY'S

PRELIMINARY REPORT

ON THE

STATUTORY LAWS

ONTARIO, NEW BRUNSWICK, AND NOVA SCOTIA,

PRESENTED TO THE HOUSE OF COMMONS.

OTTAWA:

PRINTED BY I. B. TAYLOR, 29, 31, & 33, RIDEAU STREET.

1871.

CONTENTS.

—:0:—

A.

	PAGE
Absconding Debtors	107
Actions, Personal } Limitation	91
Actions, Real } of	95
Admiralty	25
Administrators	33
Affidavits, &c. }	141
Affirmations abroad. }	
Agents	51
Appeal, Court of	26
Apprentices	138
Arbitration	72
Arrest	82
Assembly Legislative	56

B.

Bills of Exchange	118
Bills of Sale	144
Bastardy	133

C.

Children, illegitimate	133
Civil cases witnesses	104
Concealed debtors	107
Corporations	111
Courts, Superior	19
„ Admiralty	25
„ Chancery	19
„ County	24
„ Division	24
„ Error and Appeal	26
„ Magistrates	24
„ Marriage & }	24
„ Divorce }	
„ Probates	24
Crown debtors	48

D.

Debtors, Absconding }	107
and Concealed }	
Debtors, Crown	48
Debt, arrest for	82
Division Court	24
Distress for Rent	79

E.

Exchange, Bills of	118
Ejectment	77
Elections, Legislative	56
Equity	19
Error, Courts of	26
Executors and Administrators	33
Estates, Intestate	45
Estates, Lunatic	127
Evidence	104

F.

Fisheries, Sea & River	41
Foreclosure	101
Frauds, Statute of	148

I & J.

Illegitimate Children	133
Infants	135
Interest	45

I. & J.

	PAGE
Intestacy	67
Imprisonment for debt	82
Joint Tenants	44
Jury Laws	9
Justices of the Peace, Courts of	24

L.

Landlord and Tenant	76
Legislature, Elections to	56
Limitations, Statute of	90
Loans, Interest on	45
Lord's Day	53
Lunatic Asylums	130
Lunatics, Estates of	127
Lunatics, Dangerous	130

M.

Marriage, Solemnization of	115
Married Women, Assurances by	30
Married Women, Rights of	29
Magistrates' Courts	24
Master and Servant	52
Marriage and Divorce	24
Members, Election of	56
Minors and Apprentices	138
Mortgages, Personal Property	144
Mortgages, Sale of Land	101
Muncipalities	121

P.

Partition	124
Parties to suit Witnesses	104
Partnerships	37
Personal Actions, Limitations of	91
Probate Courts	24
Promissory Notes	118

R.

Real Estate, Sale of	101
Real Actions, Limitation of	95
Reference to Arbitration	72
Rent, Distress for	79
Registration of Bills of Sale	144
Rivers and Streams	41

S.

Sale, Bills of	144
Sabbath, Profanation of	53
Sale of Lands	101
Seamen	86
Sea and River Fisheries	41
Servants	52
Streams	41
Superior Courts	19

T.

Tenants, Joint and in Common	44
Tenant, Ejectment of	76
Tenant holding over	78

W.

Wills	61
Witnesses Abroad	98
Witnesses, Parties to Suit	104

PRELIMINARY REPORT

Of Hon. J. H. GRAY on the Uniformity of the Statutory Laws of the Provinces of Ontario, New Brunswick and Nova Scotia.

OTTAWA, 9th February, 1871.

SIR,—Having been requested by you to examine the laws of the Provinces of Ontario, New Brunswick and Nova Scotia, with a view to preparing for a Commission, hereafter to be issued for the uniformity of the laws of those three Provinces, under the 94th section of the British North America Act of 1867, in accordance with the provision made by Parliament to that effect. I have the honor to enclose a report of the progress made with reference thereto.

The plan finally adopted has been to gather together the statutes in each Province, bearing upon any particular subject, omitting, as a general rule, those subjects on which the Dominion Parliament, under the Union Act, has an exclusive right to legislate, such as the Criminal Law, the Militia Law, Navigation and Shipping, &c., subjects on which uniformity could be secured without the action of the Local Legislatures, but, nevertheless selecting from those subjects, one, Bills of Exchange and Promissory Notes, as coming within the daily operations of the merchants and traders of the three Provinces, for the purpose of illustrating the differences in some of the most ordinary branches of business.

The next step was to make a summary of the provisions in each Province bearing on the subject selected, placing the same in parallel columns, giving as nearly as possible the corresponding sections of the Acts of each Province, with the substance of each section, for facility of reference, and in a general column of remarks at the close, pointing out the difference. In some instances where the mode of legislation was so entirely dissimilar, as hardly to admit of a selection of corresponding sections, then to give a concise review of the main parts of the mode adopted in each Province.

In carrying out this plan it was found that while both in Nova Scotia and Ontario, the statutes had been revised up to a much later period, and that in both an available index to their statutes to within the last four or five years could be found, yet in New Brunswick there had been no revision since 1854, and no general index for sixteen or seventeen years.

First.—It, became, therefore, necessary to prepare such an index. This was done. A copy is annexed.

Secondly.—As there were many of the Imperial Statutes, which affected the Dominion —were frequently referred to in the courts—governed the administration of justice, and bore upon the property and civil rights of the three Provinces, of which statutes no collection had been made or existed in any compact form in any of the Provinces ; it was thought advisable to make one, briefly referring to them by their titles and subject matter, when they were not of a character frequently to be cited ; when they were, by giving the sections in full, as well as the title and subject matter ; but omitting all parts of the statute not bearing upon British North America. This was done. A copy is annexed.

Thirdly.—Applications were made to the Provincial Secretaries of the Provinces of

1

Nova Scotia and New Brunswick, and to the Secretary of State for the Dominion, to obtain, if possible, a sufficient number of copies of the codified and uncodified laws of the two former provinces, and of old Canada— to be used for cutting out the extracts for the parallel columns—leaving simply the general remarks to be written, thus saving labor and time, and greatly facilitating the readiness with which the comparisons could be made.

From Nova Scotia no copy of the Consolidated Statutes was obtained, but one set of the Acts for five years, from 1864 to 1869, was sent.

From the Secretary of State for Canada, one copy of the Consolidated Statutes, and the Acts passed subsequently up to the time of Confederation.

From New Brunswick, nothing but the Acts passed since Confederation ; of the laws of the latter province I had a perfect set of my own, which obviated the difficulty ; and of those of Nova Scotia, I obtained the use of the Revised Statutes belonging to the Secretary of State for the Provinces.

Fourthly.—The Statutory Laws of Ontario, irrespective of any made by the Dominion Parliament, are found in the Consolidated Statutes of Canada, up to 1859 ; the statutes passed by the United Parliament of Canada, from 1859 to 1867 ; the Consolidated Statutes applicable to Upper Canada alone, passed by the United Parliament up to 1859, and similar statutes passed by the same Parliament from that period to 1867, and the statutes passed by the Legislature of Ontario since 1867, making an approximate total, in round numbers, of 1,600 Acts or chapters ; but omitting those subjects that come exclusively within the scope of the Dominion Parliament, and have been legislated upon, and such Acts as were applicable to Quebec alone, about 1,100.

Fifthly.—The Statutory Law of Nova Scotia will be found in one volume. The revised Statutes, 3rd series, up to 1864, and in the Acts of the Local Legislature from that period, passed annually, comprising as above about, 700 Acts or chapters.

Sixthly.—In New Brunswick, the Statutory Law will be found in the 1st and 2nd volumes of the revised statutes up to 1854, and in the several Acts of the Local Legis: lature, annually passed since that period, comprising, excluding as above, and also those in the third volume, which are called private and local Acts, and which have not been at all referred to, about 1,200 Acts or chapters.

Seventhly.—Thus, in order to determine the Legislation on any particular point in Ontario, the search extends over a period of eleven years ; in Nova Scotia of six years, and in New Brunswick of sixteen years, and for the purpose of determining the entire uniformity or differences between them on matters coming within the jurisdiction of their Local Legislatures, an examination of upwards of 3,000 Acts.

Eighthly.—The laws of Nova Scotia, as found in the Revised Statutes, are the simplest, best arranged and most easily understood. Those in Ontario, from the past position and history of that Province, as a part of old Canada, and the general and separate special local legislation that was necessary, and the changes that have been made by its Legislature since Confederation, are necessarily the most complicated and difficult to arrive at, assuming that information of the law on any subject is sought by one who, from previous knowledge, is not familiar with the legislation affecting that Province. In New Brunswick, the absence of any revision for sixteen years renders the search more intricate than in Nova Scotia, though less than in Ontario.

Ninthly.—The re-enactment in the Provinces of New Brunswick and Nova Scotia of many of the old English Statutes affecting the ordinary relations of life, such for instance, as the Statutes of Frauds, 29 Charles 2, chap. 3, and the adaptation of others, with special alterations, suited to the local wants and habits of the country, such for instance, as with reference to distresses for rent, the recovery of rents by an action for use and occupation, &c., make a knowledge of the remedies within their power, attainable by the people, and by the local magistrates who administer justice in the rural districts.

In Ontario—while as in the other two provinces—those parts of the Imperial Act 9th Geo. 4, chap. 14, rendering a "written memorandum necessary to the validity of certain promises and "undertakings," which relate to taking a case out of the Statute of Limitations, the ratification of an infant's promise after coming of age, representations as to the character and credit of a third party, being in writing, are specifically re-enacted? and a special reference is made to the Statute of Frauds, for the purpose of extending the 17th section, which relates to the sale of goods of the value of £10 and upwards; yet the provisions of the Statute of Frauds, with reference to promises for the debts or defaults of another, or in consideration of marriage, or on the sale of an interest in lands, or as to an agreement not to be performed within a year, &c., &c., do not appear to have been legislated upon, and the law in regard thereto must be sought for under the authority of chap. 9, of the Consolidated Statutes of Upper Canada, "An Act respecting "property and civil rights," which declares, "that in all matters of controversy relative "to property and civil rights, resort shall be had to the Laws of England, as they stood "on the 15th October, 1792, as the rule of decision." So also with reference to distresses for rent, or actions for use and occupation, &c., &c.

Tenthly.—In some cases the Legislation on particular subjects appears to be more limited in some Provinces than in others, probably from inadvertence, perhaps from the nature of trade. For instance, in Ontario, with reference to Bills of Exchange, there is no provision whatever for the damages, interests, costs or protests on bills drawn on persons in Asia, Africa, Australia, New Zealand, Japan, Java, the Mauritius, Sandwich Islands, Cape of Good Hope; the East Indies with their great marts of trade, Bombay, Calcutta, Madras; or China; or Smyrna, or the other parts of the Eastern Mediterranean, or any places not coming under the designation of Europe, the West Indies, the United States, or other parts of America.

This omission, no doubt accidental, does not exist in the other two Provinces.

Eleventhly.—While New Brunswick and Nova Scotia long preceded Ontario in the adoption of that great legal reform which abolished the objection to witnesses on the ground of incapacity from crime or interest, and allowed parties to be witnesses in their own causes, leaving the question to be as to their credibility not their competency; (In New Brunswick as far back as 1856. In Ontario only in 1869). Yet, in several respects, the law in Ontario is in advance of New Brunswick, and in some degree of Nova Scotia, for instance, where it relates to imprisonment for debt, to recovery of landed property; to the discouragement of litigation by the difficulties thrown in the way of speculators in flaws in titles; by the powers that the courts and judges have of compelling a reference to arbitration in suits involving long and intricate accounts, the time occupied in the trial of which would operate as a denial of justice to other parties; also in the clear and specific manner in which it disposes of the real estate of intestates, and in other points to which it is not necessary here to allude.

In many of these respects, the provisions of the law in Nova Scotia are equally excellent.

In New Brunswick, the law and its provisions relating to Juries, both for simplicity, economy, and the finality resulting from the delivery of the verdict by a majority after due time for consideration; The law relating to absconding debtors in dividing the estate fairly among the Creditors—instead of securing an absolute preference to the party, who puts the process of the law in motion—and some of the provisions of the laws, both in Nova Stotia and New Brunswick, relating to partnerships, executors and trustees, to seamen, to wills, to the property of married women, &c., might judiciously be imported into the law of Ontario.

Twelfthly.—With reference to the Courts, while an Admiralty jurisdiction and Court exist in each of the other Provinces, and under the extended powers given by a late act of the Imperial Parliament, 26 and 27 Vic., chap. 24, is influencing the administration of justice in a vast number of cases of constant occurrence in a trading and maritime community, which were almost without remedy before, and the benefit of which, under that Act can be indefinitely extended to any of the Provinces, Ontario with its vast lake trade is entirely without any such tribunal.

Thirteenthly.—In the Supreme Courts of the three Provinces, the jurisdiction is to the same extent; but in the Maritime Provinces, the Court of Chancery has been nominally amalgamated with the Courts of Common Law, and its existance as a distinct tribunal abolished.

In New Brunswick its principles and mode of procedure remain as distinct as before the amalgamation with the Courts of Common Law, the change simply being that the Supreme Court has a Common Law side, and an Equity side. The same Judge may sit in Equity to-day and at Common Law to-morrow, and his decision at Common Law to-day be restrained by his decision in Equity to-morrow.

He has no power, if, in the progress of the cause at Common Law, it is found that the party would have a remedy or relief in Equity, to apply the remedy or give the relief, it must be sought for on the Equity side of the Court.

But though equitable defences in actions at Common Law are not provided for as in Ontario and Nova Scotia, yet, by section 26 of the same Act, which made the amalgamation, it is declared, "That whenever a demurrer will lie to a Bill for
Sub. chap. 2, 2nd "want of equity, the Judge on the argument may, if the facts warrant,
vol. Revis'd. Stats. "instead of dismissing the Bill, order the remedy as at Common Law,
Page 83. "or he may make such other order as to proceeding therein on the
"Common Law side of the Supreme Court, and for the trial of the same on such terms as
"to payments of costs or otherwise, as may appear to him just."

In Nova Scotia the fusion was more complete. By chap. 123, Revd. Stats. of Nova Scotia, 3rd series, it is enacted that the Supreme Court shall have, within the Province, the same powers as are exercised by the Courts of Queen's Bench, Common Pleas, *Chancery* and Exchequer in England. By chap. 124, "Of proceedings in Equity," it was enacted
—Revd. Stat. 431—"that in that chapter the term "Supreme Court," should
Sect. 1. "include the Equity Judge and his Courts ; the term "the Court," means the
"Court of the Equity Judge, except otherwise expressed or clearly indicated ; and the
"jurisdiction expressed to be transferred to and to be exercised by the Supreme Court
"means the jurisdiction and powers of the Judge in Equity, alone, or with the associated
"Judges, and of the Judges of the Supreme Court on Circuit, and of the Supreme Court
"Bench on appeals."

"In the illness or absence of the Equity Judge, or in cases requiring attention in the
"country, the duties imposed on him shall be exercised by the other Judges, as the
Sect. 2. "case may require."

"The Supreme Court has jurisdiction in all cases formerly cognizable by the Court
"of Chancery, and exercises the like powers and applies the same principles of
Sect. 3. "equity as justice may require, and as has formerly been administered in that
"Court. In all cases in the Supreme Court in which matters of Law and Equity arise,
"the Court before which they come for consideration, trial, or hearing, shall have power
"to investigate and determine both the matters of Law and Equity, or either, as may be
"necessary for the complete adjudication and decision of the whole matter according to
"right and justice, and to order such proceedings as may be expedient and proper ; and
"all writs issuable out of Chancery now issue out of the Supreme Court.

"The plaintiff may unite several causes of action in the same writ, whether they be
"such as have heretofore been denominated legal or equitable, or both. The causes
Sect. 7. "of action so united must accrue in the same right, and affect all the parties to the
"action, and must not require different places of trial."

When applicable, the practice of the Supreme Court was to be observed, when not,
the practice of the English Court of Chancery, and by section 10, "In the
Sect. 10. "final decision of cases on equity principles, the Court shall give judgment
"according as the very right of the cause and matter in Law shall appear to them, so as
"to afford a complete remedy ' upon equitable principles applicable' to the case. And in
"Sect. 43, it is declared lawful for the 'plaintiff in replevin or a defendant in
Sect. 43. "any cause in the Supreme Court, in which, if judgment were obtained, he
"would be entitled to relief against such judgment, on equitable grounds, to plead the
"facts which would entitle him to such relief.'" And the plaintiff may reply an avoidance of these facts on equitable grounds. And in ejectment, an equitable defence may be set up.
Immediately following this Act (by chapter 125), provision was, notwithstanding,

made for a distinct Equity Judge, who was to make rules to govern the practice in Equity before him, and to hear and determine all matters of Equity jurisdiction, and to preside in the Court when business required, and in the absence of the Judges of the Supreme Court from Halifax, to perform all the duties there that might be required of a Judge of the Supreme Court.

There was to be an appeal from his decisions to the Supreme Court, in which he was to sit as one of the Judges of Appeal. He was also to sit in Supreme Court in Banc., and at Chambers, but not to preside at trials or on circuit, except in cases of illness of a Judge, or other sufficient cause.

In full Bench, in cases civil or criminal, legal or equitable, the Chief Justice was to preside ; the Judge in Equity next to him, and, in case of the Chief Justice's absence, to preside.

Two years afterwards, in 1866, by 29 Vic., chap. 11, amending chapters 124 and 125, the above four sections, 1, 2, 3, 7, of chapter 124 were repealed, and the Equity Court 29 Vic.. ch. 11. and jurisdiction again re-established. Sect. 7 enacts, "That the 'Su-Sect. 7. "preme Court,' and 'the Court,' and the 'Judges' or 'Judge,' in such "chapter, except when herein otherwise expressed, or when inconsistent with the enact-"ments hereof, are confined, in all cases of exclusive chancery jurisdiction, to the Court "of the Equity Judge, or the Court or Judge occasionally exercising the equity jurisdic-"tion ; and in all cases of concurrent jurisdiction, those terms apply alike to such Court "and Judge, and to the Supreme Court and its Judges ; and in all cases purely at "Common Law, contradistinguished from chancery jurisdiction, those terms mean the "Supreme Court and its Judges alone ; and all suits or other proceedings for the "redemption or the foreclosure of mortgages under the 24th section, and for specific "performance under the 25th section ; and in relation to real estates of infants, under the "sections from the 51st to the 55th, both inclusive, of said chap.(124); and all proceedings, "matters and things relating to the custody, care, and disposal of persons of unsound "mind, and their estates and effects, under the sections from 2 to 9, both inclusive, of "chap. 152 of the Revd. Statutes ; and also, all proceedings under chap 131 of the Revd. "Statutes, third series, 'of trusts and trustees,' are under the equity jurisdiction only, "and shall be prosecuted and conducted accordingly ; and the terms, 'the Supreme Court,' "and 'the Court,' and the 'Judges,' or 'Judge,' used in the said sections and chapter, "mean the Equity Judge, or the Equity Court, or the Court or Judge occasionally "exercising the equity jurisdiction.

"But nothing in either of the said chapters, 124 or 125, applies to or affects chapter "114 of the Revised Statutes, third series, 'Of the sale of lands under foreclosure of "'mortgages,' the proceedings under which may continue to be in the Supreme Court and "before the Judges thereof.

"In case of the illness of the Equity Judge, or in case of his absence from Halifax, Sect. 8. "either within the Province on judicial duty, or for other cause, or abroad, "and also in cases requiring attention in the country on circuit, and when the "Equity Judge does not preside, the duties imposed on him may be exercised by the other "Judges, or any of them, as the cases may require."

"The Equity Judge has jurisdiction in all cases formerly cognizable by the Court Sect 9. "of Chancery, and exercises the like powers, and applies the same principles "of equity as justice may require, which were formerly administered in that "Court."

Section 6 of chapter 124, which provided, that in the absence of the Judges of the Supreme Court from Halifax, the Equity Judge should perform all the duties of a Judge of the Supreme Court, was repealed ; and in place of it, it was enacted in section 3 of said chapter 11, 29 Vic. that the Court of the Equity Judge should "be always open, "and the other Judges of the Supreme Court or any of them, in cases, where empowered "to exercise the functions of the Equity Judge, should have the full powers of the "Court."

The right of the Supreme Court to admit of equitable defences, was still retained, section 10 says :

Section 10. " But nevertheless in all actions at law in the Supreme Court, on the
" trial or argument of which matters of equitable jurisdiction arise, that Court has power
" to investigate and determine both the matters of law and of equity, or either, as may be
" necessary for the complete adjudication and decision of the whole matter; and also, all
" actions at law, to which equitable defences shall be set up in virtue of the sections of
" this chapter, under the head " Equitable Defences," from section 43 to section 50, both
" inclusive, are, and shall continue to be tried, considered, and adjudicated by the Supreme
" Court and its Judges in the same manner as regards the said several cases respectively,
" as the Supreme Court or the Judges thereof had power to do when the Act for appoint-
" ing a Judge in Equity was passed.

" But it shall be lawful for the Supreme Court, or any Judge of that Court, before
" whom the consideration, trial, or hearing of any question of equitable jurisdiction, or any
" such mixed questions of law or equity may come, if they or he shall deem it expedient
" and conducive to the ends of justice to do so, to order the case, or any subject matter
" arising thereon, to be transferred to the jurisdiction of the Equity Judge, to be dealt with
" according to the principles of equitable jurisprudence, and the exigencies of the case."

By an Act passed, chap. 2, 1870, " To improve the Administration of Justice." It is
enacted that the Supreme Court should hereafter be composed of a Chief Justice, a Judge
in Equity, and five other puisne Judges, and that the Judge in Equity should not be
required to attend the Circuits, or sit in Banc. to hear arguments, except on appeals from
the Equity Court, when he shall sit with the others; and further, that in case of his continued absence from the Supreme Court sitting in Banc., from illness or other cause,
appeals from his decisions may be heard, and judgment pronounced as if he were present.

In Ontario the court and judges of common law and chancery, with their principles
and practice remain as separate and distinct as they ever were, save that, as in Nova
Scotia, there is a provision that a defendant or plaintiff in replevin, in any case may
plead or reply the facts, that on equitable grounds would afford relief in equity against the
judgment at law if obtained, subject to the opinion and action of the judge, whether the
same can or cannot be dealt with by a court of law so as to do justice between the
parties.

Thus, in the absence of any knowledge as to what construction may have been put
or may yet be put upon the first part of section 10, 29 Vic.. chap. 11, Nova Scotia Act
of 1866, it would seem that Nova Scotia in this respect has come back to where Upper
Canada had remained, except as to the sale of lands under the foreclosure of mortgages,
chap. 114, Revised Statutes 403, and it is thought, that in New Brunswick some material
modification of the present system will at an early day have to be adopted, either by a
more complete separation or by a more complete fusion of the courts of common law and
equity.

The latter, if judiciously accomplished, would probably be the most desirable, as those
who are compelled to seek redress in litigation, expect to obtain, and ought to obtain
justice full and complete, when it is admitted they are entitled to it, without being sent at
great expense from law to equity, and from equity to law, to find it.

Fourteenthly.—In the Courts of limited jurisdiction the distinction is more nominal
than real. Those in Ontario are the County Courts and the Division Courts, the former
having jurisdiction, subject to certain exceptions, over personal actions not exceeding $200
unliquidated damages, and $400 when the damages are liquidated, and by 23 Vic., chap.
43, in actions of ejectment where the annual value of the premises does not exceed
$200. The latter being sub-divisions of the county with certain exceptions to personal
actions of $40, and money demands of $100.

In New Brunswick they are the County Courts and the Magistrates' Courts; the
former having jurisdiction, subject to certain exceptions similar to those in Ontario, in
actions ex contractu to $200, in torts to $100, but no right to try ejectment; the latter,
or Magistrates' Courts, in actions ex contractu to $20, torts to $8. The City Court of St.
John has an exceptional jurisdiction of its own.

In Nova Scotia there are no County Courts, but the Magistrates' Courts have jurisdiction for the recovery of debts—one Justice when the dealings do not exceed $20, two Justices when the whole does not exceed $80. The jurisdiction being confined to the county where the debt was contracted, or the defendant resides.

In both Nova Scotia and New Brunswick there is a " Court of Divorce and Matri- " monial Causes," with full powers to dissolve marriages *a vinculo matrimonii*, to declare the same null and void, and to hear and determine all causes, suits, controversies, matters and questions touching and concerning marriages.

In both Provinces the Court is a branch of the Supreme Court presided over by one of its Judges specially appointed for that purpose in New Brunswick by commission under the Great Seal of the Province, and in Nova Scotia, *ex officio* by the Judge in Equity for the time being, who is for that purpose termed "the Judge Ordinary." A difficulty has arisen in New Brunswick from the Act constituting this Court, making no provision for the substitution or appointment of another Judge to act *pro hac vice* in case of the illness or absence of the Judge so appointed by commission, or his being prevented by other causes from presiding, and a Bill introduced in the Dominion Parliament to remedy the defect was lost.

In Nova Scotia, the Act passed in 1866 with reference to this Court, provided that during the illness or temporary absence of the Judge Ordinary, the Governor in Council might appoint the Chief Justice or one of the Judges of the Supreme Court to act as Judge Ordinary, and by an Act passed in 1870, this last power was further extended to meet the case of his being prevented from presiding by any disqualifying cause. If this latter Act does not come within section 91 of the British North America Act, 1867, the difficulty in New Brunswick can be removed by local legislation. This difference, there-fore, at present exists between those two Provinces on that subject. In both Provinces, powers are given to the Court to enforce its decrees, and in case of divorce on the ground of adultery, to determine whether the wife's right of dower, or the husband's tenancy by courtesy shall be divested or not.

In New Brunswick the grounds of divorce, *a vinculo*, are limited to impotence, adultery, and consanguinity within the degrees prohibited by the 32 Henry VIII., touching marriages and precontracts.

In Nova Scotia they are extended to include cruelty and precontract.

In New Brunswick there is an express provision that the divorce *a vinculo* on the ground of adultery, shall not in any way affect the legitimacy of the issue. In Nova Scotia there is no such provision—perhaps not deemed necessary. In both Provinces provisions are made for appeal from the decision of the Judge to the Supreme Court, and in New Brunswick from the Supreme Court to the Privy Council in England.

In Ontario there is no statute constituting a Court of marriage and divorce.

In New Brunswick and Nova Scotia the Supreme Court being the sole Superior Court, there is no Court of Appeal from its decisions, except to the Judicial Committee of the Privy Council in England, which, owing to the great expense attending any appellate proceedings therein, is practically of no avail to the great mass of the people in those two Provinces.

In Ontario a Court of Appeal is constituted, composed of the Judges for the time being of its Superior Courts of Queen's Bench, Chancery, and Common Pleas, with power to the Governor General to appoint any retired Judge of one of the said Courts to be the Chief Justice, or an additional Judge of the said Court of Error and Appeal.

Thus Ontario is the only one of the three Provinces which affords to the litigants therein, without resort to a distant and most expensive tribunal, the opportunity of an appeal to a Court composed of Judges other than those of the particular Court in which the complainant may justly conceive that he has been condemned or deprived of his rights contrary to law.

In Ontario the Senior Judge of the County Court is, *ex officio*, Judge of the Surro-gate Court.

In New Brunswick and Nova Scotia the Surrogate Judge of Probate is appointed directly to that office by the Governor in Council.

In Ontario, the Surrogate Court may order any question of fact, arising in any proceeding before it, to be tried by a Jury before the Judge of the Court, when such trial would take place in the County Court in the ordinary manner.

In New Brunswick and Nova Scotia, the Probate Courts have no such power.

Fifteenthly.—With reference to executors and administrators, an important provision exists both in Ontario and Nova Scotia relative to the law of evidence in suits arising out of matters with deceased parties in which issue has been joined, and a trial, or any enquiry, is being had, namely, that it shall not be competent for the survivor or survivors, being a party or parties to the suit, or their wives, to give evidence on their own behalf, of any dealings, transactions, or agreements with the deceased, or of any statements or acknowledgments made, or words spoken by deceased, or of any conversation with deceased ; but such parties may be compelled to give evidence on behalf of deceased.

This apparently fair policy has not been adopted in New Brunswick, and is not in accordance with the law in England, perhaps because it is depriving one party, without any fault of his own, of an advantage which both possessed ; and perhaps because the knowledge that such an advantage may be lost, induces parties more to reduce their agreements to writing, and thereby avoid unseemly conflicts of testimony.

In Nova Scotia, the proceedings against executors and administrators *cum testamento annexo* have been simplified on behalf of legatees by permitting actions at Common Law, and in the same Act, for enabling executors appointed trustees by a will, or trustees appointed by deed, to be relieved of their trusts or executorship by an application to the Supreme Court, or to be removed on an application in the same way by any one interested in the execution of the trust. •

In the course of this work, Mr. Butler's Alphabetical Index of the Canadian Statutes, from 1859 to 1867, has been continued so far as Ontario is concerned, from 1867 to the present day ; and the New Brunswick index, first prepared and referred to above, has also been further continued to the present time.

There are many other differences which will be observed by an examination of the schedules annexed, but it is obvious that any review of a subject so comprehensive as the legislation of three Provinces must be more or less imperfect, unless made by persons familiar with the construction put upon the Statutes of each Province by the Courts of each Province. A knowledge of the decisions of the Courts in one Province alone might very erroneously lead a party to suppose that inadvertencies or omissions existed in the Statutory Laws of the other Provinces, which an acquaintance with the decisions of the Courts of those Provinces might show was not the case, but a knowledge of which could only be obtained by their being brought forward or quoted in the discussion on those differences themselves.

Opinions of the Statutes as found in the Statute Book, without knowing how far the practical operation of those Statutes may have been extended or narrowed by the critical examination to which they would be subjected in the process of judicial enquiry, must be subject to inaccuracies.

The instructions given to me being simply to prepare for a Commission hereafter to be issued—not to recommend or propose any form or suggest any change—I have confined my labor solely to pointing out the differences; but there can be no doubt that an excellent practical Code of Law, simple in its language, easily understood, expeditious and economical in its administration, could be formed from a judicious selection of the best of the Laws of each of the Provinces by men who were severally acquainted with each.

I beg to refer you for further information to the Schedules hereunto annexed, numbered 1, 2, and 3,

And have the honor to be, Sir,

Your obedient servant,

J. H. GRAY.

To the Honorable the Minister of Justice.

EXTRACTS FROM SCHEDULES.

MEMO.—*For more detailed information on the subjects referred to, the corresponding columns and sections of the several Acts in each Province bearing thereon, together with the index of each Province, must be examined as set out separately in the several Schedules.*

As the Laws of Ontario are but little known in New Brunswick and Nova Scotia, and those of New Brunswick and Nova Scotia even less known in Ontario, without an examination of the columns, sections, and index of each Province, or reference to the printed volumes of the Statutes in the several Provinces, the information imparted in these Extracts must be more or less incomplete.

For the Criminal Law throughout the Dominion, see the Dominion Statutes.

JURY LAWS.

IN ONTARIO.

In *Ontario.*—Con. Stat. chap. 31 (22 Vic., 1859, 335) :—

All persons, with certain specified exceptions, residing in any County, City, or Local Division, over 21 years of age, of sound mind, and not infirm or decrepit, assessed for local purposes, and selected at the Annual Selection of Jurors, by the Selectors of each Township, &c., from the Assessment-Roll of the Township, &c., &c., according to a certain rate there determined on, are liable to serve as Jurors on both the Grand and Petit Jury, in all Courts of Civil Jurisdiction within the Local Division in which he resides.

The exceptions are set out in 34 classes, and embrace :—Persons 60 years of age ; Executive Council and persons in the service of the Governor ; Officers of the Provincial Government ; Clerks and Servants of the Provincial Government—of the Provincial Parliament—and Public Departments ; Inspectors of Prisons ; Wardens, Officers, and Servants of the Provincial Penitentiary ; Judges of Courts, except of Quarter Sessions of the Peace ; Sheriffs, Coroners, Gaolers, and Keepers of Lock-ups ; Ministers of the Gospel ; Members of the Law Society ; Attornies ; Barristers ; Students-at-Law ; Officers of Courts of Justice ; Physicians ; Surgeons and Apothecaries ; Officers of Her Majesty's Army and Navy on full pay ; Pilots and Seamen ; Officers of Customs, Excise, and Post Office ; Sheriffs' Officers and Constables ; County and District Treasurers and Clerks ; Collectors and Assessors ; Teachers and persons actually engaged in any educational establishment or school ; Editors, Reporters, and Printers of Newspapers ; . Railway Employees ; Telegraph Operators ; Millers ; Firemen of a regular company ; aliens and convicted criminals.

Members of the Provincial Parliament, of County Councils, and Municipal Corporations, Mayors, Reeves, or Deputy-Reeves, and Justices of the Peace, are exempted from being selected as Grand or Petit Jurors in the Inferior Courts, or at any Session of Assizes, or *Nisi Prius.*

Jurors who have served within previous two years, not to be included in list made by Selectors, if sufficient Rolls can be made up without them.

Twelve Jurors are necessary to constitute a Jury, and the verdict must be unanimous.

By the Ontario Reform Act of 1868, trial of issues of fact, by a Jury, is optional with the Plaintiff or Defendant, or at the discretion of the Judge.

The Jurors are selected by the Selectors.

The Mayor or Reeve, Town Clerk, and Assessor or Assessors, are ex-officio, the first Selectors.

2

The Selectors are to meet on the first of September in each year (if a dies non, then on the day after, &c., &c.), at the public meeting place of the Municipal Council, or some other place within the Municipality, named by the Head of the Corporation, for the purpose of selecting from the Assessment-Rolls the persons qualified and liable to serve as Jurors.

Each Selector is sworn to an impartial selection by a Justice of the Peace; two-thirds of the qualified persons on the Rolls must be selected. In case of an equality of votes in making any selection, provision is made for a casting, or double vote, being given to the Mayor or Reeve first, Town Clerk second, or Assessor of most numerous Roll, or first Assessor in case of joint Assessors.

Thirdly.—An equal number of ballots, with the number selected, is made out, names of parties selected written thereon, and one-half of the number drawn, and openly declared as each is drawn.

The necessary number being completed, the list is distributed into four divisions : first, as Grand Jurors in Superior Courts ; second, as Grand Jurors in Inferior Courts ; third, as Petit Juriors in Superior Courts, including Court of Chancery ; fourth, Petit Jurors in Inferior Courts. The distribution being in the following proportion for each division : one-twelfth for the first ; two-twelfths for the second ; three-twelfths for the third ; six-twelfths for the fourth, or as nearly as may be.

The Report (as it is called) is then to be made out in duplicate, under the hands and seals of the Acting Selectors, in a form prescribed with a written declaration subscribed, by each Selector, that he has made the selection to the best of his judgment, pursuant to the Act.

One of such duplicate reports is to be filed on or before the 15th September, with the Clerk of the Peace of the County ; the other, with the City or Township Clerk. The loss or destruction of one duplicate to be supplied by certified copy of the other.

The Clerk of the Peace of the County is to keep a "Jurors' Book," and transcribe therein, between the 15th September and the 10th November, in alphabetical order, from the report of the Selectors, the names and additions of the persons selected as Grand or Petit Jurors, to be transcribed in four Rolls, according to above distribution.

On or before the 31st December, he is to deposit a certified copy thereof with the Clerk of the Crown and Pleas of the Queen's Bench in the County.

Provision is made for certified copies in cases of loss by fire, and for division of Counties after the selection.

On the first day of the Court of General Quarter Sessions in each County, held after the 10th November, the Clerk of the Peace is to bring into Court, and publicly deliver to the Chairman, sedenté curiâ, the Jurors' Book for the then next year, with the Jurors' Books of such preceding years, as may be required, and make oath in open Court, to the best of his knowledge and belief, after comparison, that the Jurors' Rolls contain a correct transcript of the persons selected, balloted and reported ; and that the other Jurors' Books are those remaining on file in his office.

The oath is to be modified accordingly when Clerk has been changed, or books brought in for first time, and if there is reason to suspect tampering with the original entries, before coming into the Clerk's possession, in consequence of which he cannot make the oath, the Quarter Sessions is to enquire into the matter.

The Books having been received, the Chairman certifies the same therein under his hand and seal, and minute of the same is made by the proper officer.

The Court then proceeds to consider the probable amount of judicial business for which Jurors will probably be requisite, in order to determine whether to select a full Jury List, or a two-third or half Jury List.

If a full Jury List is determined on, it would be :—

      1st. From the Roll of Grand Jurors, Superior Courts........ 48
      2nd. From the Roll of Grand Jurors, Inferior Courts 96
      3rd. From the Roll of Petit Jurors, Superior Courts........... 144
      4th. From the Roll of Petit Jurors, Inferior Courts.......... 288

If a two-third Jury is determined on, it would be :—

    1st. For the first... 38
    2nd. For the second.. 64
    3rd. For the third... 96
    4th. For the fourth... 216

If a half Jury is determined on, it would be :—

    1st. For the first... 24
    2nd. For the second... 48
    3rd. For the third.. 72
    4th. For the fourth.. 144

Special arrangements are made for the County of York.

The Jury Lists for the several Courts, for the ensuing year, are then made up as follows :

The Chairman of the Court of Quarter Sessions, the Warden, the Treasurer, the Sheriff; and by sec. 5 c. 44, A. D., 1863, the Clerk of the Peace; and in the absence of the Sheriff, his deputy; and by the Ontario Law Reform Act of 1868, chap. 6 sec. 20, the Junior Judge of the County Court, and the Mayor of any City situate in such County, are made ex-officio Selectors of Jurors from the Jurors' Rolls within their respective Counties. Any three of them a Quorum.

The Selectors are severally sworn to perform their duty before any Justice of the Peace. Entry thereof to be made in Minute Book of Quarter Sessions, in the presence of the Chairman presiding. The Court then orders proclamation for silence, while names of Jurors for next year for the County are openly selected from the Jurors' Rolls ; and secondly, for any person having objection to any name called, to come forth and state it.

The Selectors then proceed to select from the Rolls, the names of such persons as they, or a majority of them, deem the most discreet and competent for jurors, in the following manner :—

The Clerk of the Peace calls out name and place of residence, first on the list, for Grand Jurors for Superior Courts. Examination is then made to see whether such person is exempt on ground of service on previous panels, sufficiently recent to exempt. If yea, entry thereof, and cause made. If nay, his name is again called, and question put, shall he be selected ? &c. If decided affirmatively, by selectors or majority present, then Chairman asks if any one can shew cause why name should not be inserted on Jury List. If no cause be shewn, name is entered. If cause be shewn on oath by party, his agent or witness, name is not entered, but entry of exemption with grounds thereof made, and so on throughout the Rolls, until requisite number is obtained.

The Clerk of the Peace then makes up lists alphabetically, with residence and additions copied in Jury Book, with the number on the Roll, and on the Roll such number is marked as transferred to Jury List.

And such Lists, so selected and transferred, constitute the Jury Lists for next year. So soon as the four Lists are selected and transferred, the Chairman and Clerk of the Peace certify, after each, that fact, and the Jurors' Book with the List are deposited in the office of the Clerk of the Peace.

If from any cause in any County, &c., the selection pursuant to the Act is omitted, power is given to the Governor (by Ontario Law Reform Act, 1868, sec. 21, the Lieutenant-Governor), to call special sessions for the purpose.

The panel of Petit Jurors summoned to attend Court, to be not less than 48, nor more than 72, unless otherwise specially ordered by the Court or Judge who is to preside, in which case special provisions are made.

NEW BRUNSWICK.

In *New Brunswick* the Jury Law differs substantially from the Ontario Law in its most important characteristics—in the selection, in the qualification of the Jurors, in the number, and the mode of delivering the verdict in civil cases.

Every British male subject between 21 and 60 years of age, resident in a County, and possessing therein real or personal estate of the value of £100, is qualified to serve as a Grand or Petit Juror. The want of such qualification is a ground of challenge, or of excuse on the party's own oath.

By Act of 1870, challenge to the array on the ground of affinity in the summoning officer is taken away, unless the affinity is within the second degree.

The exemptions are the same as those in Ontario, with the exceptions of Editors, &c., of Newspapers, Railway Employees, Telegraph Operators and Millers, and by an Act passed in 1870, the exemption of Justices of the Peace from serving on Grand Juries, is also taken away.

In all non-incorporated Counties the Sheriff annually in the month of January prepares an alphabetical list of all persons qualified for Jurors in his County, with their additions and residences, and enters the same in a Book provided for that purpose, and returns the same to the Clerk of the Peace to be kept among the records.

In incorporated Counties, the Secretary-Treasurer prepares the lists, and files the same in his own office.

The Lists are to be made up from the Assessment List.

No person whose name is not upon the Jury List can be empanelled to try an issue in any Court of Record.

The Clerk of the Circuits notifies the Sheriff of the County when and where the Court is to be held, and the Sheriff thereupon summons 24 Grand Jurors, Grand Jurors' Panel, 24. and 21 Petit Jurors to attend, giving six days notice, and the same Petit " " 21. for any adjourned Court.

The Sheriff is paid for preparing the Jury Lists by the County Treasurer, out of County funds, such remuneration as Sessions determine.

If Sheriff is interested, or of kin, either party to a cause may have issued a *venire* to the Coroner, if he is interested, to elisors, to summon twenty-one Jurors for trial of cause, who are subject to same liabilities and penalties as other Jurors.

The Petit Jury for the trial of all civil causes, consists of seven persons ; in criminal causes, of twelve. In criminal causes the verdict must be unanimous ; in civil cases, if Jury do not agree within two hours, any five may return a verdict.

If they cannot agree, Judge may discharge them, and proceed to second trial at same sittings, or liberate the party charged, on bail.

The practice of starving the Jury is abolished on a trial ; the names are drawn from a box, until the seven unchallenged is complete. In case of default of Jurors, Judge may command Sheriff to name talesmen out of the qualified persons present.

If Judge, from the great amount of business, or any other cause, deems a second Jury necessary, he orders the same, and one is summoned, but not to attend earlier than the sixth day after opening the Court.

Coroners' and Sheriffs' Juries are in like manner limited to seven, though Coroners' Juries, with reference to inquest for crimes, will now come under the Criminal Law, and be regulated by the Dominion Act.

Nova Scotia.

In *Nova Scotia* the mode of selection is more like that of Ontario, but the Law differs with reference to the qualification of Jurors—the number, and mode of delivering the verdict in civil cases.

All persons, not within the enumerated list of exemptions, resident twelve months within the County, holding freehold, if in the County of Halifax, of the yearly value of $120, or personal property of the value of $2,000 ; if in any other County, freehold of the yearly value of $60, or personal property of the value of $1,200, shall be qualified to serve as Grand Jurors.

All persons twelve months resident within the County, owning property within the County of the value of $800, shall be qualified to serve as Petit Jurors of such County.

The exemptions are substantially the same as in the other two Provinces, with the addition of parties connected with Her Majesty's Navy Yard, Ordnance, and other Departments, Mail Couriers, sworn Electric Telegraph Operators, and the Cashiers and Accountants and Tellers actually employed in the several Banks, and persons who have served on the Grand or Petty Juries within the three previous years (unless in the latter instance, in case of a default of Jurors).

In every alternate year, the Sessions select from their number a Committee of not less than three Justices, resident in different sections of the County or District, to prepare and revise the Jury Lists; they are sworn; have free access to all public papers and accounts, prepare and revise the lists, and transmit copies thereof to the Prothonotary; and the lists are valid if a majority of the Justices appointed act in the compilation or return thereof.

The lists for both Grand and Petit Jurors, must contain the Christian and sir-names, or one or more of the initials, the trades, employments, residences, and distinctive appellations by which known, or usually called.

The Court of General Sessions in each County, from time to time, determines the number of Grand Jurors to be annually summoned for each district, &c., &c.

The Committee, after completing these lists, must give a copy alphabetically arranged to the Clerk of the Peace, and another to the Prothonotary, who are to post the same up in their respective offices for one month; and within two months from the last day of Sessions, at which they were appointed, the Committee, or a majority, must meet at the County or District Court House, to revise the lists (notice of such time being given on the lists posted up), and shall hear and decide objections as to the names therein, or the names omitted therefrom.

The lists so corrected, a copy must be signed and furnished by the Committee to the Prothonotary, and the lists are then to be held valid, notwithstanding omissions, or improper insertions of names.

The Jury Lists are to be revised by the Justices, by making a list of the Jurors who die or become exempt, or who are to be added to the lists already returned, and the lists are to be so amended accordingly, and considered the fully revised lists; but the Sessions, or a Judge of the Supreme Court, may direct the Revising Committee to make out and return fresh lists.

The lists are to kept posted up in the Prothonotary's Office, and as the Juries are drawn to serve each year, the year is marked opposite the Juror's name, and whether as Grand or Petit Juror.

The Grand Jury, in General Session, annually vote $1.50 to each of the Committee who revise, and five cents per mile travelling fees, going and returning, and ten cents per folio for copying.

Any Revising Justice knowingly putting on unqualified person, or omitting qualified person, or wilfully neglecting his duty, penalty $40 to $200.

Provision is made to meet exceptional case when Grand or Petit Jury have not been drawn for current year, and forms given for revised lists. The Revising Committee of Justices are to be chosen biennially, and some special provisions are made with reference to Halifax, St. Mary's and Guysborough.

After the return of the lists, the Prothonotary has the names of the Jurors written on ballot slips, and put in the Grand and Petit Jury Boxes respectively.

At the sitting of the Court, on the last term in each year, the Prothonotary, with two persons appointed by the Judge, draws from the Grand Jury Box in open Court, the twenty-four Grand Jurors for the ensuing year, striking out the names of those who have served within two years next preceding. The list is signed by the Presiding Judge. The Prothonotary issues the *venire* to the Sheriff twenty days before the sittings of the Court or Session at which such Jury is to attend, and the Sheriff summons them at least four days before time of attendance.

At each term of the Supreme Court, the Prothonotary draws in the same way from the Petit Jury Box the panel of the Petit Jurors, setting aside names of those who have served as Grand or Petit Jurors within two years next preceding, and those then serving as Grand Jurors, prepares list of names first drawn, obtains signature of Presiding Judge thereto, issues *venire* to Sheriff at least twenty days before term ; and Sheriff summons at least four days before opening of Court.

Grand Juries must be composed of thirteen members, and a majority of two-thirds of those present may make presentments.

The panel of Petit Jurors is twenty-four ; and two panels may be summoned in Counties, if requisite, when the term extends beyond one week, excepting Queen's and Antigonish.

In Halifax the panel is thirty-six, and special provision is made for two panels.

Grand Jurors, duly summoned, not attending, liable to penalty each day from $2 to $8.

Petit Jurors to $2, and forfeiture of day's pay.

Petit Jury for trial of civil causes to consist of nine, of whom, after four hours deliberation, seven may return verdict.

In criminal cases, twelve ; and verdict unanimous.

The practice of starving Jury abolished.

The Nova Scotia Law has been further amended by chap. 19, A.D. 1870, entitled an Act to amend chap. 136 of the Revised Statutes "of Juries," which enacts that, "From and after the passing of this Act, the Court of General Sessions in every County where the Supreme Court sits only in the Shire Town, and which is divided into districts, and has a Court of Sessions for each district, shall, at its first sitting, proceed to divide each of such districts into four sections, instead of eight sections as at present, such four sections to contain, as nearly as possible, an equal amount of population."

The Committee appointed by the Sessions, shall return separate lists, alphabetically arranged, of the persons qualified to serve as Grand Jurors, one list to be returned to the Prothonotary, and one to the Clerk of the Peace ; and the Clerk of the Peace for each district shall place the names of the Grand Jurors to be drawn for Sessions duty for such district in a Grand Jury Box, divided into four compartments, each compartment to contain all the names of Grand Jurors for one of such sections.

The Prothonotary shall place the names of the Grand Jurors for the whole County, in the Grand Jury Box, in eight compartments, each compartment to contain the names of the Jurors for one of such sections, and shall draw the names of three Grand Jurors from each of such compartments in the usual manner.

In drawing the Grand Jurors for Session's duties, the Clerks of the Peace shall draw the names of six Grand Jurors from each compartment in the usual manner.

Eight of such Jurors shall always continue in office for two years, and shall consist of the two first names drawn from each of such four compartments in each year.

After the drawing of the first of Grand Jurors, under this Act, sixteen names only, being four for each section, shall be annually drawn. This section to be applicable to Jurors for Sessions only.

The Panels of Grand Jurors for the years 1865, 1866, 1867, 1868, 1869, and 1870, are hereby legalized and confirmed, notwithstanding any omissions, errors, or irregularities in the preparations thereof, or in the proceedings connected therewith.

So much of chap. 136 of the Revised Statutes, and of chapter 8 of the Acts of 1865, as is consistent with this Act is hereby repealed.

Thus, with reference to the original formation of the selection, and the ultimate mode of the verdict, all the three Provinces differ.

In the mode of striking a Special Jury, they equally differ.

In Ontario and *New Brunswick* any party to a cause may have the issue tried by a Special Jury, as a matter of right, subject to the ultimate decision of the Court, as to the party who is to bear the expense thereof.

In *Nova Scotia*, an application must be made to Court, which upon motion—upon sufficient cause shown on affidavit, may order a Special Jury, the expense (by which party to be borne) is subject to the decision of the Judge at the ultimate taxation of costs.

In *Ontario* the applicant sues out a writ of *Venire Facias Juratores* to the Sheriff, who appoints a time and place for striking the Special Jury, at which time (four full days previous notice having been given to the opposite party) the Special Jury is struck; being taken solely from the Grand Jury Roll. Forty names, to which no objection has been made, or, if made, sustained, are drawn by the Sheriff from the Ballot Box, a reasonable time allowed to each party to make enquiry (in the discretion of the Sheriff), at the expiration of which time, each party strikes off 12, and the Sheriff returns the 16 remaining as the Special Jury, from whom the 12 for the trial are to be drawn.

In *Nova Scotia* the Prothonotary draws 36 names from the Petit Jury Box, the number is reduced to 18, who constitute the Special Jury, from whom the 9 for the trial are to be drawn—those first drawn and in attendance, being the Jury.

In *New Brunswick* the party wishing a Special Jury obtains an appointment from the Clerk of the Peace in the County where *Venue* is laid ; reasonable notice of the time and place must be given to opposite party. The Clerk attends with the Jury list last filed ; in the presence of both parties, openly selects 28 indifferent persons, gives a certified list thereof to the applicant, with appointment of time and place for final striking—each party attends—strikes out alternately until list is reduced to 14.

The Clerk makes out the list of the 14, duly certified, and delivers the same to the Sheriff, who summons them in the usual way, and from those who attend the Court, the seven are drawn who try the issue.

Similar provisions are made in each of the Provinces, for the expenses of the Juries being borne out of the Public Funds, subject to reimbursement as far as the charges upon Litigants would go—but they differ as to the ultimate source from which the payment is to come.

In *Ontario* the charge falls upon the County. The Sheriff makes out the pay-list and hands it to the Treasurer of the County, who pays the Juror the sum he is entitled to receive as certified by the list.

Certain fees paid on the entry of every cause for trial or assessment ; all fines and penalties imposed or levied in the Counties, not payable to the Receiver General or any Municipal Corporation, and fines on Jurors for non-attendance, are to be paid over to the Treasurer of the County to constitute a Jury Fund, and any deficit the County Council must raise by assessment specially provided for.

In *Nova Scotia* the charge is primarily upon the County Funds. The Prothonotary prepares the pay-list, instead of the Sheriff, and the Treasurer pays out of the County Funds. A Jury Fund is raised by certain entry fees on every cause, which are paid to the Prothonotary, and by him to the Treasurer ; but no provision is made for any specific raising of the deficit, should the fund not be sufficient ; such deficit, if any, would seem to be a general charge upon the County Funds.

In *New Brunswick* the Clerk of the Court, on the last day of the sitting of the Court, prepares the pay-list, and hands the same, together with the money received on the entry of each cause, for the Jury fees on trial, to the County Treasurer, who is, forthwith, to pay each Juror out of the County Funds the sum to which he is entitled.

The County Treasurer then forwards the List of such payment to the Provincial Treasurer, when a warrant is issued by order of the Governor in Council for the payment of the amount (less the sum received by the County Treasurer from the Clerk) to reimburse the County Treasurer for the difference so paid.

Thus, in New Brunswick the deficiency falls upon the Province : In Ontario and Nova Scotia upon the County.

In New Brunswick and Nova Scotia Petit Jurors alone are paid : in the former $1 per day with mileage ; in the latter 50 cents per day with mileage ; but Grand Jurors receive nothing.

In Ontario the Petit Jurors receive $1 per day, with mileage, and the Grand Jurors, such sum out of the County Funds as the County Council deem reasonable.

In each of the three Provinces, in a civil cause, each party to the cause may challenge peremptorily three Jurors.

By (chap. 8, Stat. 1865) Act of Nova Scotia, Revd. Stats., page 884, in amendment of Chap. 136, Revd. Stats, it is enacted that, "From and after the "passing of this Act the Courts of General Sessions in each County and District in this "Province where any Court shall sit at any time, not less than one month after the pass- "ing of this Act, shall, at their first meeting, and where such Court sits before the expira- "tion of that time, at the first meeting thereafter, divide such County or District into "eight Sections, such Sections to contain, as nearly as possible, an equal amount of "population ; and the Committee appointed by such Sessions shall return separate lists "of the persons qualified to serve as Grand Jurors, and the Prothonotary shall place "the names of the Grand Jurors in the Grand Jury Box in eight compartments, each "compartment to contain the names of the Jurors for one of such Sections."

Section 1.

Section 2. " Three Grand Jurors shall be drawn from each of such compartments "in the usurl manner."

Section 3. "Eight of the Grand Jurors so drawn shall always continue in office for "two years, and shall consist of those whose names shall be first drawn from the Grand "Jury Box in each year."

"After the drawing of the first panel of Grand Jurors under this Act, sixteen "names only, being two for each Secction, shall annually be drawn in "subsequent years in the same manner as prescribed in the first Section, who, with the "eight so remaining in office, shsll constitute the Grand Jury for the current year.

Section 4.

" After the division of the respective Counties and Districts into Sections, as here- "inbefore mentioned, so much of the chapter hereby amended as is "inconsistent with this Act is repealed."

Section 5.

SUPERIOR COURTS.

· COMMON LAW AND EQUITY.

ONTARIO.	NEW BRUNSWICK.	NOVA SCOTIA.
Con. Stat. U. C., Cap. 10, page 31.	Rev. Stat., Vol., Chap. 18, Page 72 to 104.	Rev. Stat., Ch. 123, 427, Ch. 124, 432—7.
——	Stat. of 1863, p. 44.	——
Stat. of 1866, 29 & 30 Vic., c. 40.	„ 1864, p. 20.	
	„ 1868, p. 42.	Stat. of 1866, 29 Vic., c. 11.
	„ 1854, p. 105.	
——	„ 1859, p. 14.	——
	„ 1860, p. 44.	
Con. Stat. U.C., Ch. 12–45.	„ 1855, p. 92.	Stat. of 1870, Chap. 2.
	„ 1856, p. 110.	
——	„ 1857, p. 12.	——
	„ 1862, p. 83.	
Stat. of 1865, Ch. 17–31.	„ 1856, p. 119.	Rev. Stat., Chap. 114, 403.
2nd Sess. of ditto, Chap. 28.	„ 1855, p. 100.	
	„ 1856, p. 110.	
——	„ 1867, p. 18, 43, 191.	
	„ 1868, p. 11, 41.	
Stat. of 1866, Chap. 39.	„ 1870, p. 48.	

SUPERIOR COURTS AND COURT OF EQUITY.

In the Supreme Courts of the three Provinces the jurisdiction is to the same extent but in the two maritime Provinces the Court of Chancery has nominally been amalgamated with the Courts of Common Law, and its existence as a distinct tribunal abolished.

In *New Brunswick* its principles, practice and mode of procedure remain as distinct as before the amalgamation, the change simply being that the Supreme Court has a Common Law Side, and an Equity Side.   By 17 Vic., chap. 18, 2 Vol. R.S., A.D. 1854, the Master of the Rolls was transferred to the Supreme Court, and each Judge of the Court was made a Judge in Equity as well as a Judge at Common Law.

The same Judge now may sit in Equity to-day and at Common Law to-morrow ; and his decision at Common Law of to-day be restrained by his decision in Equity to-morrow.

He has no power, if in the progress of the cause at Common Law it is found that the party would have a remedy or relief in Equity, to apply the remedy or give the relief : that must be sought for on the Equity side of the Court.

But though Equitable defences in actions at Common Law are not provided for as in Ontario and Nova Scotia, yet by sec. 26 of the same Act it is declared : " That when-" ever a demurrer will lie to a Bill for want of Equity, the Judge on the argument may " if the facts warrant, instead of dismissing the Bill, order the remedy as at Common " Law, or he may make such other order as to proceeding therein on the Common Law " side of the Supreme Court, and for the trial of the same on such terms as to payments " of costs, or otherwise, as may appear to him just."

In *Nova Scotia* the fusion was more complete. By chap. 123, Revd. Stats. of Nova Scotia, 3rd Series, it is enacted, that the Supreme Court shall have within the Province the same powers as are exercised by the Courts of Queen's Bench, Common Pleas, Chancery and Exchequer in England. By chap. 124, Revd. Stat. 431, " Of proceedings in Equity" it was enacted, that in that chapter the term "Supreme Court" should "include

Section 1.   " the Equity Judge and his Courts ; the term ' The Court' means the " Court of the Equity Judge, except otherwise expressed or clearly indicated ; and the juris-" diction expressed to be transferred to and to be exercised by the Supreme Court " means the jurisdiction and powers of the Judge in Equity, alone or with the asso-" iated Judges, and of the Judges of the Supreme Court on Circuit, and of the Supreme " Court Bench on appeals.

" In the illness or absence of the Equity Judge, or in cases requiring attention in

Section 2.   " the County, the duties imposed on him shall be exercised by the other " Judges as the case may require."

" The Supreme Court has jurisdiction in all cases formerly cognizable by the Court

Section 3.   " of Chancery, and exercises the like powers and applies the same prin-"· ciples of Equity as Justice may require, and as has formerly been administered in that " Court. In all cases in the Supreme Court, in which matters of Law and Equity arise, " the Court" before which they come for consideration, trial or hearing, shall have power " to investigate and determine both the matters of Law and Equity, or either, as may be " necessary for the complete adjudication and decision of the whole matter according to " right and Justice, and to order such proceedings as may be expedient and proper ; and " all writs issuable out of Chancery now issue out of the Supreme Court.

" The Plaintiff may unite several causes of action in the same writ, whether they be " such as have heretofore been denominated legal or equitable or both. The causes of

Section 17.   " action so united must accrue in the same right, and affect all the parties " to the action, and must not require different places of trial."

When applicable, the practice of the Supreme Court was to be observed ; when not,

Section 10.   the practice of the English Court of Chancery. And by section 10, " in " the final decision of cases on equity principles, the Court shall give judgment according " as the very right of the cause and matter in law shall appear to them, so as to afford a

Section 43.   "complete remedy upon equitable principles applicable " to the case. And

in section 43, it is declared lawful for the " plaintiff in Replevin, or a defendant in any
" cause in the Supreme Court, in which, if judgment were obtained, he would be entitled
" to relief against such judgment on equitable grounds, to plead the facts which would
" entitle him to such relief." And the plaintiff may reply an avoidance of these facts on
equitable grounds ; and in ejectment, an equitable defence may be set up.

Immediately following this Act (by chapter 125), provision was notwithstanding
made for a distinct Equity Judge, who was to make rules to govern the practice in equity
before him ; and to hear and determine all matters of equity jurisdiction ; and to preside
in the Court when business required ; and, in the absence of the Judges of the Supreme
Court from Halifax, to perform all the duties there that might be required of a Judge of
the Supreme Court.

There was to be an appeal from his decisions to the Supreme Court, in which he was
to sit as one of the Judges of Appeal. He was also to sit in the Supreme Court *in banco*,
and at chambers ; but not to preside at trials, or on circuit, except in case of illness of a
judge or other sufficient cause.

In full bench, in cases civil or criminal, legal or equitable, the Chief Justice was to
preside, the Judge in Equity next to him ; and in case of the Chief Justice's absence,
the Judge in Equity to preside.

Two years afterwards in 1866 (by 29 Victoria, chapter 11, amending chapters 124
and 125) the above four sections, 1, 2, 3, 17, of chapter 124 were repealed, and the
Equity Court and jurisdiction again re-established. Section 7 enacts " that the Supreme
29 Vict., c. 11, Court,' and the ' Court,' and the ' Judges ' or ' Judge,' in such chapter,
Section 7. " except when herein otherwise expressed, or when inconsistent with the
" enactments hereof, are confined in all cases of exclusive Chancery jurisdiction to the
" Court of the Equity Judge, or the Court or Judge occasionally exercising the equity
" jurisdiction ; and in all cases of concurrent jurisdiction, those terms apply alike to such
" Court and Judge, and to the Supreme Court and its Judges ; and in all cases purely at
" Common Law, contradistinguished from chancery jurisdiction, those terms mean the
" Supreme Court and its Judges alone, and all suits or other proceedings for the redemp-
" tion or the foreclosure of mortgages under the twenty-fourth section, and for specific
" performance, under the twenty-fifth section, and in relation to real estates of infants,
" under the sections from the fifty-first to the fifty-fifth, both inclusive, of said chapter
" (124), and all proceedings, matters, and things relating to the custody, care, and disposal
" of persons of unsound mind, and their estate and effects under the sections from two to
" nine, both inclusive, of Chapter 152 of the Revised Statutes, and also all proceedings
" under chapter 131 of the Revised Statutes, third series, of ' Trusts and Trustees,' are
" under the equity jurisdiction only, and shall be prosecuted and conducted accordingly,
" and the terms ' the Supreme Court,' and ' the Court,' and the ' Judges ' or ' Judge '
" used in the said sections and chapter, mean the Equity Judge, or the Equity Court,
" or the Judge or Court occasionally exercising the Equity jurisdiction ; but nothing in
" either of the said chapters 124 or 125 applys to or affects chapter 114 of the Revised
" Statutes, third series, ' of the sale of lands under foreclosure of mortgages,' the proceed-
" ings under which may continue to be in the Supreme Court, and before the Judges
" thereof.

" In case of the illness of the Equity Judge, or in case of his absence from Halifax,
" either within the Province on judicial duty or for other cause or abroad, and also in
Section 8. " cases requiring attention in the country on circuit, and when the Equity
" Judge does not preside, the duties imposed on him may be exercised by the other Judges,
" or any of them, as the cases may require.

" The Equity Judge has jurisdiction in all cases formerly cognizable by the Court of
" Chancery, and exercises the like powers, and applies the same principles of Equity as
Section 9. " Justice may require, which were formerly administered in that
" Court."

Section 6 of Chapter 124, which provided that in the absence of the Judges of the
Supreme Court from Halifax, the Equity Judge should perform all the duties of a Judge

of the Supreme Court, was repealed, and in place of it, it was enacted in section 3 of said chapter 11, 29 Victoria, that the Court of the Equity Judge should " be always " open and the other Judges of the Supreme Court, or any of them in cases where " empowered to exercise the functions of the Equity Judge, should have the full powers " of the Court."

The right of the Supreme Court to admit of equitable defences, was still retained. Section 10 says :

Section 10.   " But nevertheless, in all· actions at law in the Supreme Court, on the " trial or argument of which matters of equitable jurisdiction arise, that Court has power " to investigate and determine both the matters of Law and of Equity, or either, as may be " necessary for the complete adjudication and decision of the whole matter, and also all " actions at law to which equitable defences shall be set up in virtue of the sections of " this chapter under the head, " Equitable Defences," from section 43 to section 50, both " inclusive, are, and shall continue to be tried, considered, and adjudicated by the " Supreme Court and its Judges, in the same manner as regards the said several cases " respectively, as the Supreme Court or the Judges thereof had power to do when the " Act for appointing a Judge in Equity was passed.

" But it shall be lawful for the Supreme Court, or any Judge of that Court, before " whom the consideration, trial, or hearing of any question of equitable jurisdiction, or " any such mixed questions of Law or Equity may come, if they or he shall deem it ex-" pedient and conducive to the ends of justice to do so, to order the case or any subject " matter arising thereon, to be transferred to the jurisdiction of the Equity Judge, to be " dealt with according to the principles of equitable jurisprudence and the exigencies of " the case."

By an Act passed, chapter 2, 1870, " To improve the administration of Justice," it is enacted that the Supreme Court should thereafter be composed of a Chief Justice, a Judge in Equity, and five other Puisne Judges, and that the Judge in Equity should not be required to attend the circuits or sit *in banco* to hear arguments, except on appeals from the Equity Court, when he shall sit with the others; and further, that in case of his continued absence from the Supreme Court, sitting *in banco* from illness or other cause, appeals from his decisions may be heard, and judgment pronounced as if he were present.

In *Ontario*, the Court and Judges of Common Law and Chancery, with their principles and practice, remain as separate and distinct as they ever were—save that, as in Nova Scotia, there is a provision that a defendant or plaintiff in replevin, in any cause, may plead or reply the facts, that on equitable grounds would afford relief in Equity against the judgment at law, if obtained—subject to the opinion and action of the Judge, whether the same can or cannot be dealt with by a Court of Law so as to do justice between the parties.

. Thus, in the absence of any knowledge as to what construction may have been put, or may yet be put upon the first part of section 10, 29 Victoria, chapter 11, Nova Scotia Act of 1866, it would seem that Nova Scotia in this respect has come back to where Upper Canada had remained, except as to the sale of lands under the foreclosure of mortgages, chapter 114, Revised Statues 403. And, it is thought that in New Brunswick, some material modification of the present system will at an early day have to be adopted, either by a more complete separation, or by a more complete fusion of the Courts of Common Law and Equity.

The latter, if judiciously accomplished, would probably be the most desirable, as those who are compelled to seek redress in litigation expect to obtain, and ought to obtain justice full and complete, when it is admitted they are entitled to it, without being sent at great expense from Law to Equity and from Equity to Law to find it.

COUNTY COURTS, &c.

ONTARIO.	NEW BRUNSWICK.	NOVA SCOTIA.
Con. Stat. U. C., Chap. 15.	Stat. of 1867, Chap. 10.	
Stat. of 1860, Chaps. 43, 42, and 44.	——	
	Stat. of 1868, page 31.	
Chap. 14, 2nd Sess. 1863. ,, 30, ,, 1865.	——	
Law Reform Act of 1868-9, Chaprs. 6, 22 (23 reserved), Chap. 26.	Stat. of 1869, ps. 19, 33, 49.	
	——	
Stat. of 1869, Chaps. 7 & 12.	Stat. of 1870, ps. 33 and 48.	

DIVISION AND JUSTICES' COURTS.

ONTARIO.	NEW BRUNSWICK.	NOVA SCOTIA.
Division Court. Con. Stat. U.C., Chap. 19, page 136.	Justices' Court. 1st Vol. Rev. Stat., Chap.137.	Rev. Stat., Chap. 128, p. 465. ,, 126.
	2nd Vol. Rev. Stat. 325.	Stat. of 1866, Chap. 13.
	Stat. of 1854, p. 59, 107. ,, 1856, p. 121. ,, 1859, p. 82. ,, 1860, Chap. 37. ,, 1862, p. 18 & 84. ,, 1864, p. 24, 25 & 26. ,, 1865, p. 51 & 64. ,, 1866, p. 11. ,, 1868, p. 11 & 43. ,, 1869, p. 23 & 75. ,, 1870, p. 9 & 169.	

COUNTY COURTS, &c.

In *Ontario* the Courts of more limited jurisdiction are the County Courts and the Division Courts, the former having jurisdiction subject to certain exceptions over personal actions, not exceeding $200, unliquidated damages, and $400 when the damages are liquidated, and by 23 Vic. chap. 43, in actions of ejectment, when the annual value of the premises does not exceed $200.—The latter (being subdivisions of the County) with certain exceptions to personal actions of $40, and money demands of $100.

In *New Brunswick* they are the County Courts having jurisdiction (subject to certain exceptions similar to those in Ontario), in actions *ex contractu* to $200, *in torts* to $100, but no right to try ejectment.

And the Magistrates' Courts, the latter having jurisdiction in actions *ex contractu* to $20, *in torts* to $8.

The City Court of Saint John has an exceptional jurisdiction of its own.

In *Nova Scotia* there are no County Courts, but the Magistrates' Courts have jurisdiction for the recovery of debts. One Justice when the debt does not exceed $20 ; two Justices when the whole does not exceed $80, the jurisdiction being confined to the County where the debt has been contracted, or the defendant resides.

In *Ontario* the Senior Judge of the County Court is *ex officio* Judge of the Surrogate Court.

In *New Brunswick and Nova Scotia* the Surrogate Judge of Probates is appointed directly to that office by the Lieutenant-Governor in Council.

PROBATE COURTS.

In *Ontario* the Surrogate Court may order any question of fact arising in any pro-ceeding before it, to be tried by a Jury before the Judge of the Court, when such trial would take place in the County Court in the ordinary manner.

In *New Brunswick* and *Nova Scotia* the Probate Courts have no such power.

COURT OF DIVORCE AND MATRIMONIAL CAUSES.

In both *Nova Scotia and New Brunswick* "the Court of Divorce and Matrimonial "Causes," has full powers to dissolve marriages "*a vinculo matrimonii*," to declare the same null and void, and to hear and determine all causes, suits, controversies, matters and questions touching and concerning marriages.

In both Provinces the Court is a branch of the Supreme Court, and presided over by one of its Judges.

In *New Brunswick.*—Appointed specially for that purpose by commission under the Great Seal, and being the only Judge constituting that Court, the law vesting no power in the Government to appoint any other judge or person, to act *pro hac vice*, or in his illness or absence.

In *Nova Scotia* it is presided over by the Judge in Equity for the time being, who is for that purpose termed the Judge Ordinary, and becomes *ex officio* the Judge of that Court; During his illness or temporary absence, or in cases where he may be disqualified from acting in any cause (Act 1870, chap. 22), the Lieutenant-Governor has power to appoint under his hand and seal, the Chief Justice, or one of the other Judges of the Supreme Court to act as Judge Ordinary in his place.

In both Provinces powers are given to the Court to enforce its decrees, and in cases of divorce on the ground of adultery, to determine whether the wife's right of dower, or the husbands tenancy by the courtesy shall be divested or not.

In *New Brunswick* the ground of divorce *a vinculo*, are limited to impotence, adultery and consanguinity within the degrees prohibited by the 32 of Henry the 8th, "touching marriages and pre-contracts."

In *Nova Scotia* they include the above, and are extended to cruelty and pre-contract.

In *New Brunswick* there is an express provision that the divorce *a vinculo*, on the ground of adultery, shall not in any wise affect the legitimacy of the issue.

In *Nova Scotia* there is no such provision—perhaps not deemed necessary.

In both Provinces provisions are made for appeal from the decision of the Judge to the Supreme Court, and in *New Brunswick* from the Supreme Court, to the Privy Council in England.

In *Ontario* there is no statute constituting a Court of Marriage and Divorce, the Parliament not having yet delegated the power of divorce to any tribunal.

COURTS OF VICE-ADMIRALTY.

In *New Brunswick*, and *Nova Scotia* the Courts of Vice-Admiralty, and also for the punishment of piracy and other offences committed on the high seas, exist by virtue of the Imperial Acts and authorities, and have been in full operation in both Provinces for very many years.

The practical utility of these Courts has been material increased by a late act of the Imperial Parliament. The 26 and 27 Vic, chap. 24, entitled "An Act to facilitate " the appointment of Vice-Admirals, and officers in Vice-Admirality Courts in Her Majesty's " possessions abroad, and to confirm the past proceedings, to extend the jurisdiction, and " to amend the practice of those Courts," (passed 8th June, 1863.)

This Act provides for the establishment of Vice-Admiralty Courts ; confirms those now existing, or hereafter to be established in British possessions abroad ; specifies those now existing in a schedule to the Act, and among them the Courts at Quebec, Halifax, in New Brunswick, in Newfoundland, in Vancouver Island, and other places.

In possessions where Vice-Admiralty Courts now exist—in case of a vacancy in the Judgeship—it provides, that the Chief Justice or the principal judicial officer shall be *ex officio*, the Judge of the Vice-Admiralty Court, until formal appointment is made by the Admiralty, on the recommendation of the Local Government, to one of Her Majesty's principal Secretaries of State.

Sections 10 and 11, in addition to all the existing jurisdiction which the Court had, gives it further jurisdiction over wages, claims for disbursements, pilotage, towage, salvage, damages from collision, bottomry, &c., mortgage claims between owners for necessaries, or in respect of building, &c., equipping, &c., in possessions where no owner is domiciled, in breaches of the regulations of Her Majesty's navy at sea, in droits of the Admirality, &c., and whether the cause of action arose within or without the jurisdiction.

An appeal is given from the final sentence or decree to Her Majesty in Council—in case of improper taxation or charges by Practitioners to the High Court of the Admiralty in England.

In *Ontario* there is no Vice-Admiralty Court.

Since the passing of the Imperial Act of 26th and 27th Vic., chap. 24, above referred to, the powers and provisions of the Vice-Admiralty Court have been further greatly extended, and its utility much increased. The County Courts in England have been clothed with Admiralty jurisdiction. On this subject see the following Acts, viz : 30 and 31 Vic., chap. 45, "An Act to extend and amend the Vice-Admirality Courts Act, 1863 " (passed 15th July, 1867). Also 31 and 32 Vic., chap. 71, conferring Admiralty jurisdiction on the County Courts, (passed 31st July, 1868.)

Also 31 and 32 Vic., chap. 78, to amend the law relating to proceedings instituted by the Admiralty, and for other purposes connected therewith, (passed 31st July, 1868.)

32 and 33 Vic., Chap. 51, to amend the County Courts (Admirality jurisdiction), Act 1869, and to give jurisdiction in certain maritime cases.

Also 33 and 34 Vic. chap. 45, for establishing a District Registrar of the High Court of Admiralty in England at Liverpool, 1st August, 1870.

Many of the Provisions of these Acts might be well introduced into Ontario and the other Provinces.

4

COURT OF ERROR AND APPEAL.

The Provinces of *New Brunswick* and *Nova Scotia* have no Local Courts of Error and Appeal from the decision of their Supreme Courts. The Appellant must go to the Judicial Committee of the Privy Council in England.

No difference can therefore be pointed out, *the Province of Ontario alone* of the three Provinces, having a Court of appeal within its own territory accessible to litigants therein.

MARRIED WOMEN.

ONTARIO.	NEW BRUNSWICK.	NOVA SCOTIA.
Cap. 73, Con. Stat. U. C., .Page 791.	2 Vol. Rev. Stat., c. 114, p. 294. ——— Stat. of 1869, Cap. 33, p. 70.	Stat of 1866, Cap. 33 p. 67.

MARRIED WOMEN, RIGHTS, &c.

In *New Brunswick* the property of a married woman acquired before, or accruing, after marriage (otherwise than from her husband while married), cannot be made available for her husband's debts, or be disposed of, or encumbered by him, and in case of desertion or abandonment by her husband—or her living separate and apart from him, not willingly and of her own accord—or being compelled to support herself, she can maintain an action in her own name for debts due to her, or damages to herself, or her separate property ; at the same time, no power is given to her of alienating her property without his consent, except in the case of property acquired by her after desertion by her husband.

In 1869, by chap. 33, this protection was extended to the case of married women living apart from their husbands, not willingly, or of their own accord, although the husband may not have abandoned or deserted her, and she is now authorised, under such circumstances, to dispose of property thereafter acquired, by will, devise, gift, or grant, as if a *femme sole*, and to appoint executors to her will.

By the 2nd section of this last named Act, the husband acquires no estate right, or interest in any property real or personal, earned or acquired by her after separation for such cause, and she may convey the same in her lifetime to any person without his assent, or his being a party to the conveyance. (Chap. 114, Revis. Stat., and chap. 33, 1869.)

In *Ontario* (Con. Stat. chap. 73) a married woman holds all her real and personal property belonging to her before marriage, or acquired after marriage, free from the debts, control, or disposition of her husband, as fully as if she were sole and unmarried. If she lives apart from him for any justifiable cause, and which would not absolve him from liability for her support—cruelty, lunacy, imprisonment in the Penitentiary, habitual drunkenness, profligacy, neglect or refusal to support, desertion or abandonment ; or, if her husband has never been in the Province, she may obtain an order for protection from the Recorder, Police Magistrate, or Judge of the Division Court in the city or district (as it may be) where she resides, which order entitles her to have and enjoy her earnings, and those of her minor children, as if sole. She may dispose of her property by will, executed in presence of two witnesses, neither of whom is her husband (whether such property was acquired before or after marriage) to her children, issue of any marriage, and failing issue, then to her husband, or as she may see fit, but the husband is not deprived of any right he may have acquired as tenant by the courtesy.

Thus between *Ontario* and *New Brunswick* there are several important differences.

1st. With reference to property acquired after desertion or abandonment, or separation for the causes enumerated, or coming within the definition of the terms of the Act, the husband's tenancy by the courtesy, in Ontario would exist.

In *New Brunswick*, it clearly would not, with reference to any property acquired after desertion or separation, and a point might be raised on the construction of the 3rd section of the Act of 1869, whether, after desertion, it would exist, with reference to her separate property owned or acquired before marriage (otherwise than through him).

Secondly, if living apart from her husband, for any of the causes mentioned, in *New Brunswick*, she can maintain an action in her own name, for the enforcement of her rights, or the redress of injuries, and her husband has no power or control over the action or the claim, and cannot discharge, release, or abate it, or the action in any way or degree.

No provision to that effect is made in Ontario, and it is a question, therefore, how far the protection, as against the husband, is complete.

Thirdly, with reference to any property acquired after desertion or separation as aforesaid, *in New Brunswick* a married woman may convey it, or will it as she pleases.

In *Ontario* it would be a question whether she could convey it at all, and her power to will it, is limited as above mentioned.

Fourthly, in Ontario the intervention of a Magistrate is necessary to give the right.

In *New Brunswick* it attaches at once, by virtue of law.

In both Provinces the separate property of a married woman is made primarily liable for her debts contracted before marriage, and for judgments obtained against her husband for her torts.

In *Nova Scotia* the law differs from that of both of the other Provinces ; up to 1866 there does not seem to have been any Statute as to the rights of a married woman in her separate property, or its protection from the debts or liabilities of her husband, or of disposal by him.

The Act of 1866, 29 Vic., Chap. 33 is confined entirely to the case of married women deserted by their husbands. It is not as comprehensive in its provisions as the Law in *Ontario* and *New Brunswick*.

When deserted by her husband, she may, after such desertion, apply to a Judge of the Supreme Court, for an order for protection against her husband and his creditors. If the Judge is satisfied of such desertion, that it was without reasonable cause, and that the wife is maintaining herself by her own industry or property, he may give an order protecting her earnings and property acquired since the desertion, and such earnings and property shall then belong to her as if a *femme sole*. Such order must be entered with the Registrar of Deeds, within which whose Jurisdiction the wife resides.

This order, as in *Ontario*, is open to be rescinded, by an order of a Judge, on sufficient cause shewn, on an application by her husband or any creditor, or person claiming under him. But, while it remains in force, it protects and renders and preserves valid, both during its continuance, and after its discharge should one be obtained, all dealings that may be, or have been had with the wife, during such desertion, and without knowledge of such discharge.

The Act further gives the wife, pending the continuance of such order, the rights of sueing and of being sued, as if she had obtained a divorce, and also, if any of her property is seized or held by the husband, or any creditor, or person claiming through him, the power of bringing an action to restore the specific property, and also a sum equal to double the value of the property so seized—if seized or held after notice of the order.

In other respects it does not interfere with the ordinary law as to the marital rights of the husband in the wife's property.

MARRIED WOMEN, ASSURANCES BY.

Substantially the same.

EXECUTORS AND ADMINISTRATORS.

ONTARIO.	NEW BRUNSWICK.	NOVA SCOTIA.
Con. Stat. U.C., Cap. 78, 806,	2nd Vol. Rev. Stat., c. 29, 359.	Rev. Stat., Cap. 143—610.
Cap. 15, Stat. of 1863 (2nd Sess.) p. 72.		Cap. 145, Rev. Stat., sec. 10.
Cap. 28, Stat. of 1865, 2nd Sess., p. 143.		Cap. 7, 1865, p. 881—3.
Cap. 10, Stat. of Ontario, 1868 and 1869, p. 40.		Cap. 7, Stat. of 1869, p. 39.
Cap. 37, Stat. of Ontario, 1868 and 1869, p. 229.		
Cap. 18, Stat. of 1869, p. 36.		

EXECUTORS AND ADMINISTRATORS.

In *Ontario* and *Nova Scotia*, in proceedings by or against the representatives of a deceased party, the law does not permit the survivors (or their wives) on either side, if parties to the suit, to give evidence on the trial or inquiry, on their own behalf; but such survivor, &c., may be made a witness by the representatives of the deceased, on behalf of the deceased.

In *New Brunswick* there is no such restriction on the Law of Evidence.

In *Nova Scotia*, legatees may sue the Executor at Common Law for legacies. Residuary Legatees being Co-Executors, may also sue each other at Common Law for their rateable parts, and Executors may also be removed on application to the Supreme Court, and other Executors or Trustees may be appointed in the place of those removed by the Court, or any two Judges thereof.

No such statutory power exists in *Ontario* or *New Brunswick*.

In *Ontario* there is a provision, that in case of the death of one joint contractor, proceedings may be had against the representative of deceased, as if the contract had been joint and several, notwithstanding the other contractor may be still living, and action be pending against him. (Cap. 78, sec. 6.)

In *New Brunswick* and *Nova Scotia* there are no provisions to this effect.

In *New Brunswick*, Executors or Administrators, Plaintiffs or Defendants, may bring their actions or be prosecuted within six months after death—if party dies before limitation of time—or within thirty days thereafter, if cause of action survives. (1 Vol. Rev. Stat. 141.) And in the same Province under the provisions of the Act relating to the Administration of Justice in Equity, (2d Vol. Rev. Stat. 84, sec. 31.) a summary power is given to a Judge on an application on the Equity side, by a creditor, next of kin, or person interested in a Will, after cause heard on summons and affidavits, to make an order in his discretion for the administration of the estate, real or personal, when the whole estate has been by devise vested in a trustee for sale, and for receipt of rents and produce—which order is to have the force of a decree.

In *Ontario* and *Nova Scotia* these provisions are not found.

The powers as to distresses for rent, and bringing actions for injuries to real or personal property by or to the deceased in his lifetime, with the limitations within which such proceedings must be taken, are similar.

In Nova Scotia, by the amending statutes of 1865, chap. 7, an excellent provision is made for a Trustee, Executor, or Administrator, to obtain the opinion or advice of a Judge in Equity, respecting the management or administration of the trust property, or the assets of any testator or intestate, a proceeding which may sometimes save a good deal of wasteful litigation, and render unnecessary the injudicious interposition of personal legislation by parliament in matters of a private nature.

Sec. 7.—By sec. 7, it is enacted, " Any Trustee, Executor, or Administrator shall " be at liberty, without the institution of a suit, to apply by petition to the Judge in " Equity, for the opinion, advice, or direction of such Judge on any question respecting " the management or administration of the trust property, or the assets of any testator or " intestate ; such application to be served upon, or the hearing thereof to be attended by " all persons interested in such application, or such of them as the said Judge shall think " expedient. And it shall be in the power of the said Judge to direct any question " arising on any such applications to be argued before him, and to appoint counsel for that " purpose, if he shall think it necessary to do so. And he is also empowered to " refer questions arising on such applications to the consideration and judgment of " himself, with two Judges of the Supreme Court associated with him, or the Bench of " the Supreme Court, and to direct the argument to be had before the said Associated or " full Court. The Trustee, Executor, or Administrator acting upon the opinion, advice, " or direction given by the said Judge in Equity, or Associated Court, or Supreme " Court, shall be deemed, so far as regards his own responsibility, to have discharged his

5

" duty as such Trustee, Executor, or Administrator, in the subject matter of the said
" application ; provided, nevertheless, that this act shall not extend to indemnify any
" Trustee, Executor, or Administrator in respect of any act done in accordance with such
" opinion, advice, or direction, as aforesaid, if such Trustee, Executor, or Administrator
" shall have been guilty of any fraud, or wilful concealment, or misrepresentations, in
" obtaining such opinion, advice, or direction ; and the costs of such application, argu-
" ments, and counsel, as aforesaid, and the party or funds by, or out of which they shall
" be paid, shall be in the discretion of the Judge in Equity, or Associated Court, or
" Supreme Court."

A similar provision was made in *Ontario*, in 1865, under the title, " An Act to
"Amend the Law of Property and Trusts in Upper Canada," only it requires that such
application should have the certificate of counsel as to the propriety of the appli cation.
No such statutory provision is found in *New Brunswick*. Of course in that
Province the opinion or decision of a Court, may be obtained by means of an amicable
suit ; but in cases where no such arrangement can be come to, the Estate may be wasted
before the Law is declared, and the Trustee, Executor, or Administrator be in no way
to blame.

PARTNERSHIPS.

ONTARIO.	NEW BRUNSWICK.	NOVA SCOTIA.
Con. Stat. Canada, c. 60, Limited Partnerships, 689.	1 Vol. Rev. Stat., c. 121–305.	Rev. Stat., c. 80—312.
Con. Stat. U.C., c. 78, sec. 6.	Do do c. 137, sec. 37.	Stat. of 1865, c. 10, R. S. 886.
Con. Stat. U. C., c. 19—149.	C. 19 p. 65, Statutes of 1858.	
Statutes of Ontario, 33rd Vic. 1869, c. 20—39.	C. 31 p. 49, Statutes of 1860. page 105.	
	Statutes of 1864, p. 105.	
	Winding-up Act of Incorporated Companies.	

PARTNERSHIPS.

In the three Provinces, the Acts relative to limited partnerships, the rights and liabilities of special partners therein, the distinction in such partnership between special and general partners, the provisions for signing and filing the certificate of partnership and its terms, with the Registrar of Deeds of the County, or the Clerk of the County Court, as the case may be ; the provisions in case of dissolution or insolvency, and other matters arising out of such partnership, are substantially the same, excepting that in New Brunswick in case of assignment by such partnership or insolvency, it is expressly provided that Crown debts shall first be paid or secured, and there is no provision—as in Ontario and Nova Scotia—expressly excluding a special partner from ranking on the estate, or claiming as a creditor until the claims of all other creditors of the partnership are satisfied.

Con. Stat. Canada, chap. 60, 689 ; N. B., R. S., chap. 121 ; N. S., R. S., 3rd Series, Chap. 80.

In *Nova Scotia.*—In the same Chapter 80, are some excellent provisions for winding up the affairs of a partnership consisting only of two persons, which has terminated, and the parties cannot agree.

It provides that either may file a petition in the Supreme Court, stating the facts respecting their dealings, and praying the aid of the Court. Thereupon a summons is served with a copy of the petition on the partner complained against. On the return and proof to the Court, that the partnership consisted of two persons only, the Court by rule orders each partner to select an arbitrator. If the partners do not within the time specified in the rule, select two arbitrators, the Court appoints two ; those two select another, and the three are, by law, the arbitrators to settle the partnership dealings. Before commencing, the arbitrators are sworn fairly to settle the business.

They then order production of books, papers, &c., and appoint time and place for investigation, and examination of partner and witnesses ; and if either party fails to attend, arbitrators proceed *ex parte.*

The arbitrators have power to summon witnesses, and administer oaths, and shall examine the partners and their witnesses on oath. They or any two of them, are to make their award, with or without costs, in their discretion ; file the same in the Prothonotary's Office, and judgment is thereupon to be entered at the next term, if no sufficient objection be shewn ; which judgment is to be final, and execution may be issued thereon.

The arbitrators, or any two of them, may order the costs of the proceedings, including a reasonable compensation for themselves, to be paid by either of the partners, and in such manner as the arbitrators, or any two of them may direct ; and the Court is to enforce such payment by attachment or otherwise.

After such adjudication by the arbitrators, no proceedings in Equity, touching the partnership dealings by one partner against the other, will be allowed.

There exist no provisions of this nature for winding up a partnership in *Ontario* or *New Brunswick.*

In *New Brunswick*, the 21st Vic. chap. 19, A. D. 1858, was passed reciting as its object, to promote, and secure greater confidence in dealing with co-partnerships, and facilitating the recovery of debts, by making accessible the names of the different persons composing firms:

It required that all persons then carrying on business in co-partnership in the Province as general partners, should within six months after passing the Act, severally make and sign a certificate containing the names and places of residence of the partners in the firm ; and that all firms thereafter to be established, should, previous to carrying on business in the Province, do the same.

That such certificates should be proved or acknowledged in the same manner as deeds or conveyances of land, and should be filed in the office of the Registrar of Deeds for the County, where the business was, or was to be carried on.

That, on dissolution or changes, similar certificates were to be proved and filed ; that the Registrars of Deeds should receive and file the certificates so proved, &c., and enter the same in a Record Book to be kept for that purpose, for which entry he should be entitled to a fee of 1s. 3d.

The Book to be open at all times to inspection on payment of a fee of 1s.

That such certificates, as soon as filed, should be published in the *Royal Gazette* for two consecutive weeks.

Penalties of £15 for omitting to make, file and publish the certificate; and a further penalty of £2 10s. for each days' neglect in omitting to do so, after notice from a creditor, or any persons dealing with the firm, are imposed, and are made recoverable by the Clerk of the Peace, for the use of the County.

The rights of third parties, as against the firm, were not to be affected by the Act; and provision was made, that copy of the certificate filed, certified by the Registrar, should be *prima facie* evidence of the co-partnership.

In *Ontario and Nova Scotia*, there is no Act of this nature establishing penalties; and in *New Brunswick* it is comparatively nugatory—the right of third parties not being affected, no private prosecution for the penalty being given, and the fine, when collected, going to the County, no one seeks to enforce the penalties, and certificates are not filed as required by law.

RIVERS AND STREAMS.—SEA AND RIVER FISHERIES.

Ontario.	New Brunswick.	Nova Scotia.
Con. Stat. U. C., c. 47—459. ——— Stat. of 1866, of Municipal Inst., c. 51, sect. 280. ——— Stat. of Ontario, 1867–8, c. 30—180.	1 Vol. Rev. Stat., c. 101, „ „ c. 64—147. ——— Statutes of 1856, p. 108. „ 1858, p. 83. „ 1860, p. 61 & 77. „ 1861, p. 28. „ 1862, p. 83. „ 1863, p. 30.	Rev. Stat., c. 103. ——— Statutes of 1870, c. 6.

Vide Dominion Act, 31st Vic., c. 60, 1868, 177.

RIVERS AND STREAMS.

In both *Nova Scotia* and *New Brunswick* rivers are, by statutory enactment, declared to embrace streams, creeks, or brooks.

In *Nova Scotia*, on the application of twenty freeholders, resident in the locality of any river, or owning lands thereon, or interested in lumbering thereon, or otherwise using the said river for transportation purposes—first approved of by the Sessions and Grand Jury—the Government is authorized to appoint three or four Commissioners for clearing and removing obstructions between such points in the river, as the Grand Jury and Sessions shall designate. And for that purpose the said Commissioners may enter on public and private lands, remove obstructions, erect wing-dams, and do all other acts necessary for facilitating its use for the purpose mentioned ; and they may make regulations, preventing the throwing in or falling in of slabs, refuse wood or saw-dust, from saw-mills ; and the Sessions may impose penalties therefor, and direct the mode of recovery thereof. These penalties, which were by the former Act limited from $1 to $8, are now increased by chap. 6, 1870 to, "from $8 to $40."

For the above purpose the Commissioners may borrow any necessary sum—not exceeding $4,000—and secure the repayment thereof by the imposition of tolls sanctioned by the Sessions, upon the articles brought down the river. Such tolls, however, only to last until the money borrowed, with interest, has been repaid ; and an account thereof, with the expenditure and other proceedings of the Commissioners, to be annually submitted to the Sessions for audit.

The authority so given is to sanction no claim upon the Provincial Revenue, or interference with the navigation or fisheries further than may be absolutely necessary, and not to injure or affect private rights, otherwise than as expressly provided.

The Sessions have a general power to regulate the transportation of logs and lumber on rivers, and the erection of booms, and the fees for boomage, &c.

In New Brunswick there is no law of the character of that of Nova Scotia, but the Sessions have power to make regulations for the preservation of the navigation of rivers and harbors, &c., and for preserving the banks of rivers, and for the regulations and management of booms for holding timber, &c., and for driving timber and logs, fixing tolls for boomage, &c.

And by special enactment, with reference to the sea and river fisheries, no slabs, edgings or other mill rubbish, saw-dust excepted, shall be allowed, or put in any river or stream, under a penalty varying from 10s. to £15.

The Corporation of the cities of St. John and Fredericton, have similar and further powers also with reference to the same and other subjects.

In *Ontario*, by a special Act, chap. 47, C. S., U. C., the conditions on which trees may be cut on certain enumerated rivers, are particularly set forth—sec. 1.

In case any person throws, or any mill-owner suffers, or permits to be thrown into any river, rivulet, or water-course, any slabs, bark, waste stuff, or other refuse of any saw-mill (except saw-dust), or any stumps, roots, shrubs, tan bark, &c., or any person cuts or falls any tree across any river, rivulet, or water-course, and allows them to remain, he incurs a penalty from 20 cents to $20 for each day such obstruction remains, over and above all damages, &c. (weir-dams and *bona fide* crossings, not impeding the flow of water or passing of rafts excepted). Provisions are made for the recovery of these penalties.

From this Act, the River St. Lawrence, the River Ottawa, and rivers and rivulets, "where salmon, pickerel, black bass or perch do not abound," are excepted.

JOINT TENANTS AND TENANCY IN COMMON.

ONTARIO.	NEW BRUNSWICK.	NOVA SCOTIA.
Con. Stat. U. C., cap. 82, page. 830.	1 Vol. Rev. Stat., c. 117–296.	Rev. Stat. c. 113, p. 402.

JOINT TENANTS AND TENANTS IN COMMON

The only difference between the three Provinces on this subject is that, in *Nova Scotia* the statutory provision, abolishing the distinction between Joint Tenancy and Tenancy in Common (where not otherwise specially provided in the deed, grant or will, creating the Tenancy), has a retrospective effect.

In *Ontario*, retrospective as far back as 1st July, 1834.

In *New Brunswick*, prospective only from time of Revised Statutes, 1854.

INTEREST ON LOANS.

ONTARIO.	NEW BRUNSWICK.	NCVA SCOTIA.
Con. Stat. U.C., c. 43—449.	Statutes of 1859, c. 21, p. 74.	Rev. Stat. c. 82—741.
Con. Stat, U.C., c. 58—682.		

46

INTEREST ON LOANS.

In *Ontario*, any rate of interest that may be agreed upon is legal, except—

1stly. Banks incorporated by Royal Charter, or by authority of, or established under any particular Acts of the Legislature of Canada are not to take more than 7 per cent.

2ndly. If note discounted at any bank carrying on business in Canada (Old) is payable at any other of its branch banks within the Province, other than the one at which it is discounted, the bank discounting may retain and receive in addition to the discount for defraying expenses of collection, a rate, varying from ¼th to ½ per cent., according to the time note has to run.

If payable at any other than one of its own branches or agencies, in addition to the discount, a sum not exceeding ½ per cent. to defray expenses of agency and exchange in collecting.

In the absence of any specific agreement, 6 per cent. only to be charged, and be recoverable.

Corporations, Companies or Associations (other than banks) authorised by law before the 16th August, 1858, to lend or borrow money, are forbidden upon any contract to take directly or indirectly for loan, more than 6 per cent., except when authorised by that Act (Chapter 58, Consolidated Statutes of Canada) or by some other Act or Law, and in case of so doing, contract is declared void, and Company forfeits treble the value of the loan—one half to the Government of the Province, the other half to the person suing. No limitation as to time within which action must be brought.

In *New Brunswick*, by special enactment in 1859, chapter 21, the rate of interest recoverable by law is limited to 6 per cent.—if more is stipulated for at the time of the loan, or taken, it does not vitiate the contract ; but in any action brought to enforce such contract, the excess paid beyond 6 per cent. may be deducted from the amount due upon the contract.

With reference to Banks under the Acts of the Legislature of the Province, or by Royal Charter, interest is limited to 6 per cent., if more, by any contrivance, is taken, the Bank forfeits the principal sum with all interest and profits—one half to the Queen, for the use of the Province, the other half to the person suing for the same. Action must be brought within twelve months from the time of the offence.

The Act not to extend to bottomry bonds, damages on protested bills, cases of contracts, when the penalties are mutually binding, or contracts for the hire of grain or live stock, when casualties thereto are at the risk of the lender.

In *Nova Scotia* the old law still prevails. Interest on loans is limited to 6 per cent., all contracts reserving more declared void ; and all persons taking or receiving a greater rate to forfeit treble the value of the monies or goods contracted for or secured. Contract for hire of grain or live stock, &c., and hypothecation of vessels excepted.

CROWN DEBTS AND DEBTORS.

ONTARIO.	NEW BRUNSWICK.	NOVA SCOTIA.
U. C. Statutes of 1866, c. 43, p. 139.	1 Vol. Rev. Stat., c. 5—24. C. 7—25, Stat. of 1868. 31st Vic., c. 6.	

CROWN DEBTS AND DEBTORS.

In *Ontario*, the position of the Crown as a creditor of, or holding securities from, an individual, is, by statutory enactment passed in 1866, made exactly the same as that of any ordinary person, and the distinctions previously existing in favor of the Crown, both as to the binding character of the security, and its priority in operation are done away with. A bond to the Crown or a judgment or recognizance in favor of the Crown, would not in any way bind the real or personal estate, or create any preference other than it would do in ordinary cases.

In *New Brunswick*, by special enactment, the lands of the debtor shall be bound, in cases of specialities to the Crown, from the date thereof ; and in case of simple contract debts to the Crown, from the time of signing judgment. An execution on the judgment against the goods and chattels, lands and tenements of the debtor may issue, and the sheriff, for want of goods and chattels, may levy on' the lands and tenements of the debtor, *bound as aforesaid, whether in his hands or otherwise.*

In *Ontario*, prior to 1866, there was an Act, chapter 5, Consolidated Statutes of Upper Canada, providing for the registration of securities under seal or of record containing debts due to the Crown in the office of the Clerk of the Queen's Bench at Toronto, and that such securities should not affect the lands or any interest in the lands of the persons executing the same or affected thereby, as against any subsequent purchaser, except from the date of such registration. This Act was repealed (except as to existing registered securities) by the Act of 1866, and Crown and subject put upon an equal footing.

In *New Brunswick* there has never been any such Act for registration of Crown debts. Judgments, of course, are registered in the office of the Clerk of the Supreme Court, as in all other cases ; but there is no special provision for other securities to the Crown being registered. As these securities affect lands, it has been urged that they ought to be registered in the Registry Office of the County where the lands lie, in order that purchasers might not be taken in by the existence of Crown Bonds or Securities, of which it would be most difficult for them, if not impossible, to obtain information.

It is said, on the contrary, that as such securities are given every day in Revenue cases, contracts for Public Works, and other public transactions, it would impede mercantile operations to require such registration.

The Act of 1866 settles the question in *Ontario*.

In *Nova Scotia* there does not appear to have been any particular legislation on the subject, and the Crown debts would therefore operate as at Common Law and bind the lands, &c,

In 1868, an Act was passed by the Legislature of New Brunswick, expediting the means of recovering Crown debts, and rendering more clear and specific the duties and liabilities of parties dealing with the Public Revenue, or owing the Crown, the provisions of which are set forth in the New Brunswick column. No similar enactments have been passed in Ontario or Nova Scotia.

AGENTS, CONTRACTS WITH.

ONTARIO.	NEW BRUNSWICK.	NOVA SCOTIA.
Con. Stat. Can., c. 59—684.	None.	Rev. Stat., c. 81—317.

Corresponding Sections.

ONTARIO.		NOVA SCOTIA.
1 & 2		1
3		2
4 5 6		3
7 & 8		4 & 5
9		6 & 7
10 & 11		8
12 & 13		9 & 10
15 16 17		11 12 13
18 19		14
20		15
Not 14 21 22.		Not 16

MASTER AND SERVANT.

ONTARIO.	NEW BRUNSWICK.	NOVA SCOTIA.
Con. Stat. U. C., c. 75—798.	None.	Rev. Stat., c. 123—424.
Stat. of 1865, 2nd Sess., 29 Vic., c. 33—152.		

AGENTS, CONTRACTS WITH.

In *Ontario* and *Nova Scoiia*, the Statutes on this subject are substantially the same. In *New Brunswick*, there is no Statute.

MASTER AND SERVANT.

In *New Brunswick*, there is no particular enactment regulating master and servant· The matter is left to the ordinary law in the same manner as other contracts, but there is a Statute regulating minors and apprentices.

In *Nova Scotia*, the law under its title, professes to apply to master and servant, but does not refer to questions of domestic service &c. It is like the law in *New Brunswick*, regulating minors and apprentices.

In *Ontario* it seems more general though it is evidently intended, mainly to regulate questions of manual labour, and of journeymen engaged in any trade or craft.

THE LORD'S DAY, PROFANATION THEREOF.

ONTARIO.	NEW BRUNSWICK.	NOVA SCOTIA.
Con. Stat. U.C., c. 104–943.	1 Vol. Rev. Stat., c. 144–411.	Rev. Stat., cap. 159.

THE LORD'S DAY, PROFANATION THEREOF.

The provisions for punishing the profanation of Sunday or the Lord's Day in Upper Canada are laid down with great precision, and are extremely strict and minute. C. 104, C. S. U. C.

They are to be enforced by penalties varying from one to forty dollars on conviction before a single Justice, on the oath or affirmation of one witness, or on view had by the Justice himself. One moiety of the penalty to be paid to the party charging the offence in writing before the Justice, and the other to the Treasurer of the County, and on non-payment of the penalty with costs, imprisonment for three months, but the party making the charge in writing shall not be admitted as a witness. There is a saving clause in the Act, that it is not to extend to people called Indians. This Statute if enforced must be very effective.

In *Nova Scotia* and *New Brunswick*, the Statutes on this subject are not so numer-ous in their provisions or so minute, the terms are more general, the penalties are not to exceed Forty Shillings, or four days imprisonment.

In *Nova Scotia* and *New Brunswick*, the Statute of 29 Charles II cap. 7 sec. 1, which enacts "that no tradesman workman, laborer, or other person shall do or exercise "any worldly labor, business, or works of *their ordinary calling* upon the Lord's Day, or "any part thereof, works of necessity and Charity alone excepted," has been held to be in force.

In Upper Canada, Section 8 of the above Act (C. S. U. C., c. 104.) declares, that all sales and purchases and all contracts, for sale or purchase of any real or personal property whatsoever, made by any person or persons on the Lord's Day, shall be utterly null and void.

The Dominion Act, Chap. 36, 1869 "respecting the Criminal Law and repealing " enactments therein mentioned," leaves the Acts in the three Provinces on this subject untouched, except Sections 1 and 3 of the Nova Scotia Act, which had reference to disturbing persons assembled for Religious Worship, or for any moral, social, or benevolent purposes.

ELECTIONS TO THE LEGISLATIVE ASSEMBLIES.

ONTARIO.	NEW BRUNSWICK.	NOVA SCOTIA.
Statutes of 1868–9, 32 Vic., c. 21.	Statutes of 1855, c. 37.	Rev. Stat., c. 28—757,
Statutes of 1868–9, 32 Vic., c. 4, page 14.	Statutes of 1858, c. 33.	C. 2—5.
	Statutes of 1859, c. 32–150.	Stat. of 1870, c. 24.
	Statutes of 1870, c. 21, p. 18.	

ELECTION LAWS.

In the three Provinces the Election Laws differ very materially, both as to the qualification of the Electors and the Candidates, the mode and time of voting, and the restrictions imposed upon the Exercise of the Franchise.

First :—As to the qualification of the Voters.

In *Ontario*, every male person 21 years of age, a British subject, by birth or naturalization, not coming under any legal disqualification, duly entered on the last revised and certified List of Voters, being actually and *bona fide* the owner, tenant, or occupant of real property of the value hereinafter mentioned, and being entered in the last revised Assessment-Roll for any city, town, or village, as such owner, tenant, or occupant of such real property, namely :—

In Cities, of the actual value of $400
In Towns   "   "   300
In Incorporated Villages, of the actual value of 200
In Townships,   "   "   200

shall be entitled to vote at Elections for Members for the Legislative Assembly.

Joint owners or occupiers of real property rated at an amount sufficient, if equally divided between them, to give a qualification to each, shall each be deemed rated within the Act ; otherwise, none of them shall be deemed so rated.

" Owner " means in his own right, or in right of his wife, of an estate for life or any greater estate.

" Occupant," *bona fide* in possession, either in his own right or in right of his wife, (otherwise than as owner or tenant) and enjoying revenues and profits therefrom to his own use.

"Tenant" shall include persons who, instead of paying rent in money, pay in kind " any portion of the produce of such property."

In *Nova Scotia* every male subject by birth or naturalization, 21 years of age, not disqualified by law, assessed on the last revised Assessment-Roll, in respect of real estate to the value of $150, or in respect of personal estate, or of real and personal together, of the value of $300, shall be entitled to vote.

Also, when a firm is assessed in respect of property sufficient to give each member a qualification, the names of the several persons comprising such firm shall be inserted in the List, but no member of a corporate body shall be entitled to vote or be entered on the Section 22. list in respect of corporate property.

Also, when real property has been assessed as the estate of any person deceased, or as the estate of a firm, or as the estate of any person and son or sons, the heirs of the deceased in actual occupation at the time of the assessment, the persons who were partners of the firm at the time of the assessment, and the sons in actual occupation at the time of the assessment shall be entitled to vote, as if their names had been specifically mentioned in the assessment, on taking an oath, if required, in accordance with the facts coming Section 57. within the separate classification of the above provisions.

In *New Brunswick* every male person 21 years of age, a British subject not under any legal incapacity, assessed for the year for which the Registry is made up :—In respect of real estate to $100, or personal property, or personal and real, amounting to $400, or on an annual income of $400, shall be entitled to vote.

Thus, in both Nova Scotia and New Brunswick the Franchise is more extended than in Ontario. In Ontario it still savors of the real estate. In New Brunswick and Nova Scotia it is based upon personal estate, *per se*, as well as real estate.

In *Ontario* certain persons are forbidden to exercise the Franchise whether qualified or not, namely :—Judges of the Supreme Courts, of County Courts, Recorders of

8

cities, Officers of the Customs of the Dominion, Clerks of the Peace, County Attorneys, Registrars, Sheriffs, Deputy Sheriffs, Deputy Clerks of the Crown, Agents for the sale of Crown Lands, Postmasters in Cities and Towns, and Excise Officers, under a penalty of $2,000, and their votes being declared void.

Again, no Returning Officer, Deputy-Returning Officer, Election Clerk, or Poll Clerk, *and* no person who at any time, either during the Election, or before the Election, is, or has been employed in the said Election, or in reference thereto, or for the purpose of forwarding the same, by any Candidate, or by any person, whomsoever, as Counsel, Agent, Attorney, or Clerk at any Polling Place at any such Election, or in any other capacity, whatever, and who has received or expects to receive, either before, during, or after the said Election, from any Candidate, or from any person, whomsoever, for acting in any such capacity, as aforesaid, any sum of money, fee office, place, or employment, or any promise, pledge, or security, whatever therefor, shall be entitled to vote at any Election.

No woman shall be entitled to vote at any Election.

In *New Brunswick* and *Nova Scotia* there is no restriction as to the exercise of the Franchise by persons who are duly qualified. On the contrary, express provisions are made to enable presiding Officers, Poll Clerks, Candidates and their Agents, when acting in the discharge of their various duties connected with the Election, to poll their votes in districts where, otherwise but for such provisions, they would not be entitled to vote.

As to the Qualification of Candidates.

In *Nova Scotia* the Candidate must possess the qualification requisite for an Elector or shall have a legal or an Equitable freehold estate in possession, of the clear yearly value of eight dollars.

In *New Brunswick* the Candidate must be a male British subject, 21 years of age, and for six months previous to the test of the writ of Election have been legally seized as of freehold for his own use of land in the Province of the value of £300, over and above all incumbrances charged thereon.

In *Ontario* by the Act of 1869, 33 Vic., chap. 4, passed to amend the Act of the previous Session, entitled : "An Act respecting Elections of Members of the Legislative "Assembly" (the 32 Vic., chap. 21,) it is enacted "That from and after the passing of "that Act, no qualification in real estate should be required of any Candidate for a seat "in the Legislative Assembly of Ontario ; any Statute or Law to the contrary notwith-"standing, and *every such last mentioned Statute and Law is hereby repealed.*"

Neither the said 32 Vic., chap. 21, nor the preceding Acts of the same Session, chaps. 3 and 4, defining the privileges, immunities and powers of the Legislative Assembly, and for securing the Independence of Parliament, point out what shall be the qualifications of a Candidate, and the previous Acts in the Consolidated Statutes on the subject have been repealed.

By the 23rd sec. of 32 Vic., Chap. 21, 1869, the Electors present on Nomination Day are to name the person or persons whom they wish to choose to represent them in the Legislative Assembly. There is no restriction as in Nova Scotia, that a Candidate must have the qualification of an Elector, which, among others, is that he shall be a male subject by birth or naturalization, or, as in New Brunswick, specifically, that he must be a "male British subject."

In the Ontario Act 32, Vic., chap. 21, sec. 4, it enacts "No woman shall be entitled "to vote," but there is no restriction in the 23rd section as to the sex of the person or persons whom the Electors shall choose to represent them in the Legislative Assembly, nor is there any clause in the two Acts, chaps. 3 and 4, before referred to, from which any such restriction can be inferred. The 61st sec. of 32 Vic., chap. 21, declares "That "no Candidate shall, with intent to promote *his* Election, provide or furnish, &c." But by the General Interpretation Act, passed by the Legislature of Ontario, Chap. 1, 31st Vic., (1867-8) sec. 6, clause 8, it is enacted that "words importing the singular number,

'' or the *masculine* gender shall include more persons, parties, or things of the same kind " than one, and *females* as well as males, and the converse."

And by the 3rd sec. of the same Act the interpretation clauses were to apply to all Acts thereafter passed.

Thus it would appear, that if the Electors present on Nomination Day choose a female as a Candidate, and, in case of a Poll being demanded, she should be Elected, she would be entitled to take her seat as a Member in the Legislature of Ontario.

In this respect Ontario differs from the other two Provinces, and may be said to be in advance of both England and the United States on this point.

In all three of the Provinces persons holding offices of profit or emolument under the Crown, excepting Members of the Executive Government, are debarred from holding seats in the Assembly. In all the three Provinces there must be a registration of Voters, -the foundation in all being the same, namely—the Assessment List of the District—tho details for the Register of Voters, simply varying according to the qualifications which give the vote, and which entitles the Voter's name to be put upon the List—the exceptional instances in Nova Scotia being when the representatives of a deceased party, or the members of a firm assessed are entitled to vote ; and in New Brunswick, when there has been no assessment in the parish for the year for which the List ought to be made up.

In Ontario the voting is *viva voce.*

In New Brunswick and Nova Scotia—By Ballot—introduced in Elections in New Brunswick in 1855 ; in Nova Scotia in 1870.

The Mode of Conducting the Election.

The mode of conducting the Election by ballot is very much the same in Nova Scotia as it is in New Brunswick, the most material distinction between the two being that in the several Polling Districts in New Brunswick the Ballots are openly counted at the close of the Poll at each Polling Place, in the presence of the Candidates, or their Agents, duly added up openly in the presence of all parties, entered in the Poll Books or Check 'Lists' signed by the Poll Clerk, and countersigned by the Candidates or their Agents, and the Ballots then forthwith destroyed, the countersigned Poll Book or Check List with a written statement of the result of the Poll at that District, with the signatures of the Candidates or their agents is then forthwith enclosed, sealed up, and publicly delivered to the presiding officer to be transmitted to the Sheriff to be opened on Declaration Day.

Whereas, in Nova Scotia the Ballot Boxes, with the Ballots, are sealed up and sent. This mode was in accordance with the Law first introducing the Ballot in New Brunswick, but, being found liable to abuse, was subsequently amended as above mentioned.

In Nova Scotia—The 17th sec. of the Act of 1870, introducing the Ballot, abolishes the Public Meeting held by the Sheriff on Nomination Day, but he is to attend at the Court House, or other place prescribed, between 11 a.m. and 2 p.m., for the purpose of receiving the names of the Candidates, and he shall exclude all persons not having business in connection with the Election.

In Ontario and Nova Scotia, in case of a General Election, the Polling must be simultaneous throughout the whole Province.

In New Brunswick it is not so ; the Sheriff or the presiding Officer for the County or City selects such time within the writ as he deems most suitable for the convenience of the Electors within his County.

WILLS.

NEW BRUNSWICK.	NOVA SCOTIA.	ONTARIO.
1st Vol., Rev. Stat., c. 110, 276.	Rev. Stat., c. 112—397.	Con. Stat. U. C., c. 73, sec. 16.
Vide Married Women, Stat. of 1869, c. 33.		c. 82, sec. 13.
		Statutes of 1869, page 36.

WILLS.

In *New Brunswick*, a testator may, by his will, dispose of all property, and rights of property, real and personal, in possession or expectancy, corporeal or incorporeal, contingent or otherwise, to which he is entitled, either in law or equity, at the time of the execution of his will, or to which he may expect to become at any time entitled or be entitled to at the time of his death, whether such rights or property have accrued to him before or after the execution of his will.

In *Nova Scotia*, the same.

In *Ontario*, there is no provision of this general character, but by the Consolidated Statutes of Upper Canada, chapter 82, section 11, real estate, acquired subsequently to the execution of a will, would pass under a devise conveying such real estate as testator might die possessed of.

In *New Brunswick* and *Nova Scotia*, a testator must be twenty-one years of age.

In *Ontario*, there is no provision to this effect.

In *Nova Scotia*, a married woman may, with the consent of her husband testified in writing, make a will of her personal property; a will of real and personal property to which she may be entitled in her own right, or for her separate use, and wills in a representative character. The last three, not in the language of the statute having the husband's assent appended to the clause.

It is presumed there must have been in Nova Scotia some judicial construction upon this section.

In *New Brunswick*, a married woman's right to make a will is left exactly as it was before passing of the Act, chapter 110, 1st volume Revised Statutes, 1854, and the husband's assent is therefore requisite, except in case of desertion by her husband, when the right of disposal of property acquired by herself after desertion without his assent, might be presumed from 3rd section, chapter 114, 1st volume Revised Statues " of the " real and personal property of married women."

On this latter point, however, all doubt has since been removed, and the power greatly extended by Act of 1869, chapter 33rd. *Vide* Remarks—Married Women.

In *Ontario*, it is specifically enacted that after the 4th May, 1859, a married women may make a will, in presence of two witnesses—neither of whom is her husband—of her separate property, real and personal, to her children, and failing issue, then to her husband, or as she may see fit, as if *sole;* but husband's tenancy by the courtesy is not to be affected. Consolidated Statutes, Upper Canada, 794, 22 Vict., chapter 73, section 15.

The mode of the execution of wills in New Brunswick and Nova Scotia is the same. They must be in writing, executed by the testator at the foot thereof, or his signature thereto acknowledged by him in the presence of two witnesses, present at the same time, and attesting in his presence and the presence of each other; but in New Brunswick, there is a further provision that though not signed at the foot thereof, its execution shall be deemed good, if it be apparent, from the will and position of the signature, or from the evidence of the witnesses thereto, that testator intended it as his last will.

In *Ontario*, there is no general statute as in Nova Scotia and New Brunswick, with reference to wills ; but in the Consolidated Statutes, Upper Canada, chapter 82, section 13, it is provided that any wills affecting lands, executed after 6th March, 1834, in the presence of and attested by two witnesses, shall be as valid as if in the presence of three, and attested by three, and it is sufficient if such witnesses subscribe in presence of each other, though not in the presence of the testator ; in this latter respect differing from the laws of the other Provinces as well as from the law of England.

The Imperial Act of 7th, William IV. and 1st, Victoria, chapter 26, in amendment of the law with respect to wills, puts an end to the power existing under the pre-existing law, which infants male at 14, and infants female at 12, had of disposing by will of personal property (*vide* Jarman) ; but as this Statute does not operate in Canada, and there is no local Act on the subject, the law in this respect, in Ontario, differs from the law in New Brunswick and Nova Scotia.

In *New Brunswick* and *Nova Scotia*, soldiers in service and seamen at sea may dispose of their personal estate as before, and in Ontario, by section 83, chapter 16, the Act regulating Surrogate Courts, the same provision is made with reference to soldiers and seamen, with the addition that no nuncupative will made after that Act came in force should be good (5th December, 1859); this latter provision was not necessary in New Brunswick and Nova Scotia, as it was there enacted that all wills should be in writing, saving the exception just named.

In *New Brunswick* and *Nova Scotia*, wills executed as provided under their Statutes, are valid without publication.

In *Ontario*, there is no such statutory provision. (Memo. It has been held in England that it is not necessary—though Hardwick, Chancellor, had previously decided that it was —of freehold lands. *Vide* Jarman, 1st volume, 74.)

In *New Brunswick* and *Nova Scotia*, incompetency of witnesses (by reason of interest arising from devise or legacy) to the execution of the will has been removed. The will is not thereby rendered invalid or incapable of proof. The witnesses are admitted, and, if proved, the will is declared valid ; but the devise or legacy is made void, even if it be to the husband or wife of witness.

In *Ontario*, there is no statutory provision of this character (the Act, chapter 13, 1869, of the Ontario Legislation to amend the Law considered below); and while the Imperial Act 25th George II., chapter 6, which makes void the devise or legacy to the witness himself is in operation in Ontario, the 1st Victoria, chapter 26, extending the same consequence to a devise to the wife or husband of the witness, is not.

In *New Brunswick*, creditors, whose debts are by the will charged upon the estate, are not incompetent as witnesses.

In *Nova Scotia*, similar provision.

In *Ontario*, none, but would come in under George II., chapter 6.

In *New Brunswick*, no witness is rendered incompetent by reason of his being declared executor.

In *Nova Scotia*, the same.

In *Ontario*, no similar provision.

In both New Brunswick and Nova Scotia, objections as to the competency of witnesses in all legal proceedings (and, therefore, necessarily in the proof of wills) arising from interest or crime have long been removed by the Acts allowing parties to a cause to be witnesses ; but those Acts in no way affect the provisions in the Acts relating to wills which declare legacies and devises to such parties void.

In *Ontario*, the law on this subject is apparently in a somewhat anomalous position. There are no such provisions relating to wills in any of the statutes which refer to wills, and it may be a question whether under the Act passed by the Ontario Legislature in December, 1869, entitled: "An Act to amend the Law of Evidence in Civil Cases," which removes the incompetency of witnesses arising from crime or interest, the difficulty of the question would be removed.

Under the English Law as prevailing before 1st Victoria, chapter 26, whether a will of freehold estate attested by a witness, whose wife or husband had an interest in the will Jarman, as devisee or legatee, would be invalid or not, was to some degree uncertain, 1st., 67-'8. though if the devise or legacy had been to the witness himself, under 25th George II., chapter 6, the doubt as to the invalidity is removed, because it clearly makes him competent, and declares the devise or legacy void. The Statute, 1st Victoria, chapter 26, repealed the 25th George II., chapter 6, except as to the Colonies in America, extended the removal of the incompetency of the witness, and the forfeiture of the devise and legacy to the husband or wife of the witness as well as to the witness himself, and to Jarman, 67. personal estate as well as real estate (it having been decided that the 25th George II., chapter 6, did not extend to wills of personal estate), but the 1st Victoria, chapter 26 is not in force in Canada, and equivalent provisions to those in New Brunswick and Nova Scotia have never been enacted in Canada.

The Statute of Ontario of December, 1869, which admits an interested witness to give evidence, says nothing about devises or legacies to witnesses to wills being void. Thus, in the absence of any knowledge, as to what may have been done by the Courts of Upper Canada on this subject, it would appear that on the first point as to the validity or invalidity of a will of freehold, witnessed by one to whose wife or husband a devise or legacy has been left (under the Statute, George II), the question remains open; secondly, if the devise or legacy was to the husband or wife of the witness, it would not be affected at all if the will was sustained ; and thirdly, it having been decided that that statute did not apply to personal property, a person directly interested by a legacy to himself, or his wife, in sustaining a will, may be admitted as a witness to prove the will creating the interest without forfeiting or affecting the legacy—a principle inconsistent with the policy of the same Act (Ontario, December, 1869), which, while allowing parties to a cause, or interested in its results, to give testimony in their own favor, yet, in an action brought by or against executors or administrators, excludes the testimony of the survivor, as to what may have been said or done to him by the deceased, whose representatives are the other party to the suit ; thus, the testator being dead, a claimant who is a witness to a will of personal property, might prove the document, giving to himself or his wife £500 ; but in a suit brought by him to recover £5 from the testator's estate, he would not be admissable as a witness to prove that the testator promised to pay him £5.

The 1st Victoria, chapter 26 has been substantially re-enacted in New Brunswick and Nova Scotia ; not so in Ontario.

The revocation of a will by a subsequent marriage, and its non-revocation by a change of circumstances, or otherwise, than by a will or codicil duly made, is the same in all three Provinces.

In *New Brunswick* and *Nova Scotia*, obliterations, interlineations, or alterations made in a will after its execution (except when the words or effect of the will before alteration is not apparent) shall have no effect, unless alteration is executed as required for a will ; and no will or codicil which has been revoked is to be revived, otherwise than by a duly executed will or codicil reviving it.

In *Ontario*, no such provisions.

In all three Provinces, a conveyance of a part of an estate made after the execution of a will, is not to affect the operation of the will upon the part not conveyed.

In *Ontario* and *New Brunswick*, both with reference to real and personal estate, the will is to be construed as if executed immediately before the death of the testator.

In *Nova Scotia* the same provision exists, and there is also a clause that executors are to be trustees for the conveyance of real or personal property contracted to be sold, though the same may have been disposed of in the will.

In *New Brunswick* and *Ontario*, there is no clause of this latter character. Such a case would be left the operation of law either by a bill for specific performance, or an action on the contract for damages.

In *New Brunswick* and *Nova Scotia*, specific provisions are made, that devises failing, become part of the residuary estate ; a devise of freehold to comprehend leasehold, when no freehold existed answering the description in the will ; and the provisions with reference to the execution of powers of appointment as to real and personal estate are the same in both Provinces.

In *Ontario*, none.

In all three Provinces it is provided that devises of real estate without words of limitation, pass the freehold or the entire estate of the testator, unless the contrary clearly appears from the will.

In *New Brunswick* and *Nova Scotia*, similar provisions with reference to the lapsing of estates-tail or quasi-entail, in case of the death of the devisee during the lifetime of the testator, leaving inheritable issue, are made, declaring that such devise shall not lapse, but take effect as if the death of the devisee had happened immediately after the death of the testator.

In *Ontario*, none. •

In *New Brunswick*, there is an express provision that a devise of real estate to a trustee without any express limitation of the estate to be taken by him, and without any remainder over after the trust has been executed, shall vest in the trustee the fee simple or other entire legal estate of the testator, and not an estate determinable after the trust has been satisfied.

In *Nova Scotia* and *Ontario* there is no such provision.

In *New Brunswick* and *Nova Scotia*, provision is made that a devise to a child, who dies in the lifetime of the testator leaving issue, shall enure to the benefit of the issue.

In *Ontario*, none.

In *New Brunswick* and *Nova Scotia*, provisions are made for the construction of the words in a will.

In *Ontario*, none.

In the three Provinces, wills affecting lands must be registered ; but the term within which a subsequent purchaser may be affected by the non-registration varies in each.

In *New Brunswick*, if there has been suppression, or concealment, or delay arising from the will being contested, under certain circumstances the term varies from six months to three years.

In *Ontario*, under the Registry Act, 1868, chapter 20, to affect subsequent purchasers, wills must be registered within twelve months next after the death of the devisor, testator or testatrix, or in case the devisee is disabled from registering the will within the said time, by reason of its being contested, or other inevitable difficulty, without his or her wilful default or neglect, then within twelve months after attainment of the will or probate, or removal of the impediment preventing the registration.

In *Nova Scotia* there are no exceptions or provisions of this character ; but there is a provision, that for the suppression of a will, there shall be a forfeiture of £5 for every month " the offender shall suppress a will after the lapse of the first thirty days." (Section 28.)

In *New Brunswick*, there is the same penalty of £5 for any person guilty of suppressing a will, in the Act regulating Courts of Probate ; or if the executor does not prove and cause the will to be registered, or renounce his executorship within thirty days after the death of the deceased without just excuse for the default.

In all three Provinces, stealing or fraudulently suppressing or destroying a will is provided for under the head of Crimes.

INTESTACY.

ONTARIO.	NEW BRUNSWICK.	NOVA SCOTIA.
Con. Stat. U. C., c. 82.	Rev. Stat., 1 Vol., 282.	Rev. Stat., c. 115.
Statute of 1865, 2nd Sess., page 145.	Stat. of 1858, c. 26—78.	Statutes of 1865, c. 3—879.
Imp. Acts, 22 & 23 Ch. II., chap. 10, and 29 Charles II., c. 31.	1 Vol. Rev. Stat., c. 111.	

INTESTACY.

Real and Personal Estate.

In New Brunswick, the Act regulating Intestate's Estates is extremely short. 21st Vic., cap. 26, as explained by 22 Vic., cap. 25, A.D. 1858 and 1859.

As to Real Estate.

The Real Estate is to be divided equally (regard being had to advancements made before his death by Intestate, so as to make all equal) amongst the children or their legal representatives, including in the distribution children of the half-blood, reserving the widow's right as dower.

In case there be no children of the Intestate, then the next of kindred in equal degree and their representatives.

The Personal Estate (1st Vol. Rev. Stat. 283,) is apportioned one-third ($\frac{1}{3}$) to widow, residue in equal proportions among children and their representatives (*per stirpes*). The heir-at-law, notwithstanding an advancement to him of Real Estate by Intestate in his lifetime, shall nevertheless receive an equal share with the other children ; but any other child having received any such advancement, shall be entitled only to such equal share, deducting the value of his advancement.

(*Memo.*) This is the only difference at present existing in favor of the heir-at-law, and probably escaped attention when 21st Vic., cap. 26, was passed.) If there be no children, or legal representatives of them, one half goes to the widow, the residue equally to next of kin, in equal degree and their representatives ; but no representation among collaterals after brother's and sister's children.

If no widow, equally among children, and if no widow and no children, to next of kin in equal degree. (Same as 22, 23 Charles 2, cap. 10, as explained by 29 Charles 2, cap. 30.)

If after the death of the father, any of his children shall die in the lifetime of the mother, intestate without wife or children, every brother and sister and their representatives shall have equal share *with the mother.* (Same as 1st James 2, cap. 17, differing in this respect from Real Estate.)

In *Ontario.* Con. Stat. cap. 82, page 829. The Real Estate, in case of Intestacy, goes 1st. To children and their representatives, *per stirpes* in equal parts.

2nd. If Intestate, dies without descendants, *leaving a father*, the Estate will go to the father, unless the Intestate acquired it on the part of the mother, and she be living, and if *such* mother be dead, then the estate so acquired goes to the father for life, reversion to the brothers and sisters; if no brothers or sisters, or descendants, &c., to father absolutely.—Sec. 27.

If Intestate die without descendants, and without a father (or a father entitled, as under the last section), and leaving a mother, and a brother or sister, then the estate goes to the mother for life, reversion to the brother or sister, or their descendants, &c. ; and if no brother or sister, or descendants of any, then to mother absolutely.—Sec. 28.

If Intestate dies without descendants, and without father or mother, then estate goes to brothers and sisters, and their descendants, *per stirpes*, however remote.—Sects. 29, 30, 31.

If no heirs, under any of the preceding sections, then the estate, if acquired on the father's side, shall go to the brothers and sisters of the father of the Intestate, and their descendants, in equal shares, *per stirpes* (or their descendants) ; and if none on the father's side, then to those on the mother's side.—Sects. 32, 33.

If the estate should have come on the mother's side, failing heirs, &c., then to the brothers and sisters of the mother, and their descendants, per stirpes, in equal shares, &c. ; and if none on the mother's side, then to those on the father's side.—Sect. 34.

If acquired neither on father or mother's side (failing *ut ante*), then estate shall go to brothers and sisters of father and mother, alike, and their representatives, *per stirpes.*—Sec. 35.

Half-blood succeeds with whole-blood.—Sec. 36.

And, failing heirs, under all those Sections, the estate goes to next of kin, according to the rules of the English Statute of Distribution of Personal Estate.—Sec. 37.

Posthumous children to inherit as if born in lifetime.—Sec. 39.

MEMORANDUM.—With respect to *Real Estate.*

The Law of New Brunswick differs from that of Ontario in this, that while the Law of Ontario, in case of failure of lineal descendants, provides, specifically, that the estate shall go to the father or mother, or their representatives, *quoad*, the fact, from whom the estate may have been derived ; the New Brunswick Law simply provides, " that in case " there be no children of the Intestate, then it shall go to the next of kindred, in equal " degree, and their representatives."

The next of kindred would be determined by the Civil Law, and is the same as in the distribution of Personal Estate, (under 22nd and 23rd Charles II., cap. 10, as explained by 29, Charles II., cap. 30, in England, and in New Brunswick by 1st vol. Revd. Stat., page 283). And, therefore, the *mother,* as well as the father, would conjointly succeed to the Real Estate of the deceased (inasmuch, as they, being next of kin *in equal* degree, would succeed to the Personal Estate of the Intestate, who, leaving no widow, died without issue, in exclusion of his brothers and sisters) ; and, assuming the father was dead, she, being the nearest of kin, according to the Civil Law, would be entitled to the whole.

(The Stat, of 1st James II., cap. 17, which provides, that the father being dead, the mother, and brother and sisters, shall share alike, applies only to Personal Estate, and in no way alters the Rule as to who next of kin may be under the Civil Law, so that with reference to Real Estate in New Brunswick, the mother is in a better postion than she is with reference to Personal Estate.)

As to *Personal Property.*

The Law in Ontario and New Brunswick is the same ; the Stat. 22 & 23 Charles II. cap. 30, modified by 1st James, II., cap. 17, prevailing in Ontario under the Act respecting property and Civil Rights (chap. 9, page 30, Cons. Stat.) ; and in New Brunswick by specific re-enactments of their several provisions.

The Nova Scotia Law differs from both,—See revised Statutes, 3rd series, 747.

With reference to *Real Estate.*

1st. It first provides for an equal destribution among children and their descendants, per stirpes.

2nd. If no children, one-half of Real Estate goes to father ; the other half to widow, in lieu of dower ; if no widow, all to father.

3rd. If no children and no father, one-half to widow ; the other half, in equal shares, to his mother, brothers and sisters, and their representatives, and failing all these, then to next of kin, in equal degree. If there be no kindred, all to widow for her own use, if there be one. Minors unmarried, without father or mother, property to brothers and sisters in equal degree.

The Civil Law to prevail, and half-blood to inherit with whole-blood.

With reference to *Personal Property.*

1st. Widow has all her paraphernalia, apparel, ornaments, apparel of minor children, and provisions for 90 days, and such other necessaries as shall be allowed by

Judge of Probate, deceased's wearing apparel, to $40 value, to be be distributed among family by the administrator.

2nd. Residue of Personal Estate, after payment of the debts of deceased, &c., to be distributed, one-third to widow, residue to persons entitled to the Real Estate, and if no widow, all residue to the latter. (Changed from one-half, R.S. 747, to $\frac{1}{3}$ by Amend. Stats., 1865, chap. 3.)

3rd. There is a provision under the Law relating to Intestacy, that a posthumous child, unprovided for by the Testator in his will, shall have the same interest in the estate, both Real and Personal of the father, as if *the father had died intestate*, and for such purposes, all the devises and bequests made in the will shall abate proportionably.

4th. Advancements to be taken into consideration in t'.e apportionment, and if exceeding the proportion, that would come to the child on a division, he is to be excluded from the division, but cannot be called on to refund.

5th. All gifts and grants are to be deemed advancements, if stated to be so made in the gift or grant, if charged in writing as such, or acknowledged in writing, or on examination before the Judge of Probate on oath, and not otherwise.

6th.—Tenancy by Courtesy, or of a widow in dower, not affected.

Of both Real and Personal Property, by amended Statutes of 1865, chap. 3, sec. 2.— " If a married woman shall die intestate, without issue surviving, one-half of the Real and " Personal Estate owned by her, in her own right, or held by her for her separate use, " shall go to her husband, and the other half to her father ; if she have no father, then to " her mother, brothers and sisters, in equal shares; and the children of any deceased " brother or sister, by right of representation, and if there be no issue, father, mother, " brother or sister, or child of brother or sister, the whole shall go to her husband."

ARBITRATION.

Nova Scotia.	New Brunswick.	Ontario.
Rev. Stat., c.146—615.	2 Vol. Rev. Stat., 351.	Con. Stat. U. C., c. 22—216.
		Also clauses relating to do. in following pages : 128, 159, 468, 513, 529, 615, 629, 739, 749, 926, 1,014.
		Con. Stat. of Canada, 756.
		Stat. of Ontario, 1867, 186.

Corresponding Sections, Schedule 2.

ARBITRATION.

In the three Provinces of Ontario, New Brunswick and Nova Scotia, there are specific provisions by statute providing for and regulating references to arbitration, to be found in Ontario, principally in the Common Law Procedure Act 22 Vic., chap. 22. Cons. Stat. U. C. 216. In New Brunswick in a chapter consolidating the various amendments of the Law 2 vol. Rev. Stat. 351. And in Nova Scotia in a chapter exclusively on the subject. (Rev. Stat. 615.) They are in a great measure similar, but in Ontario and Nova Scotia, they are more comprehensive, and under certain circumstances give powers to the Court, or the Judges thereof, with which they are not vested in New Brunswick.

In *Nova Scotia* the power of arbitrators appointed by Rule of Court, or a submission containing an agreement that the submission should be made a Rule of the Supreme Court, shall be irrevocable, unless the Court or Judge otherwise order.

In *Ontario*, it is the same, but it is not necessary that a submission should contain any agreement that it would be made a Rule of Court, such an agreement is to be inferred unless the negative be stated, and the arbitrator is to proceed notwithstanding any attempt at revocation, and to make his award through the party making such revocation may not afterwards attend the reference.

In *New Brunswick* the power of an arbitrator appointed by any Rule of Court or Nisi Prius in any action brought in the Supreme Court is not revocable without leave, &c., &c., and arbitrator must proceed as in Ontario, but there is no provision with regard to submissions, or agreements for reference to arbitration, otherwise than by Rule of Court, as in Nova Scotia and Ontario.

The difficulty, however, has been always obviated in New Brunswick by making the submission or agreement contain such clause, and then forthwith getting it made a Rule of Court, when the Law would at once apply; but there has been no Legislation on the point, and the power of non-revocation in cases of submission by agreement, must depend upon the prudence and discretion of counsel—instead of—as in Ontario, upon the Law.

In *Nova Scotia*, arbitrators, whether appointed by rule of Court or *otherwise*, have power to issue subpoenas for attendance of witnesses at any time or place in subpoena named, and parties subpoened on tender of fees for travel, &c., as in Supreme Court, are liable for non-attendance, &c., as if the subpoena had issued from the Supreme Court.

The Arbitrators appointed by Rule of Court, or submission containing agreement that it may be made a Rule of Court, have power to administer oaths; but if the submission contains no such agreement, any Justice of the Peace may administer the oaths. No person shall be compelled to produce papers, that he would not be compelled to poduce at a trial, or to attend more than two consecutive days.

In New Brunswick it is necessary to obtain a rule or Order of the Court or Judge for attendance of witnesses and production of documents, and disobedience to order will be a contempt of Court, if appointment of time and place, be served with order. Witness is entitled to expenses as if upon trial, and not bound to attend more than two consecutive days, or to produce documents that he would not have to produce at trial. If ordered or agreed in the Rule of Reference that witnesses may be examined on oath, arbitrators have power to administer, and false evidence is made perjury.

In Ontario, the provision for the attendance of witnesses, administering the oath, expenses, documents, attendance and punishment, &c., are the same as in New Brunswick.

In Ontario and Nova Scotia, provisions are made for a compulsory reference of matters in issue, if pending a trial, or if on proper application made after suit commenced and before trial, it shall appear to the Court or a Judge, that the matters in dispute consist of matters of account which cannot conveniently be tried in the ordinary way, and the Court or Judge may direct the terms, appoint the arbitrators, in case the parties cannot agree to name them, (in number not to exceed three) and may make such other orders, as will tend to justice.

10

In New Brunswick there is no such power of compulsory reference of matters in suit.

In all three Provinces, provisions substantially the same exist for treating awards made under references as above, as the verdict of a Jury, and for enforcing the same, or setting the same aside or making application to that effect—in Ontario and Nova Scotia, by modes specifically pointed out—in New Brunswick, under the ordinary practice and rules of the Court.

In Nova Scotia and Ontario, provision is made for appointment of another arbitrator, or proceeding without, in case the one first appointed dies, or neglects or refuses to proceed, or for the appointment of an umpire, and for his proceeding in lieu of the arbitrators, in case they cannot agree, or have allowed the term for making their award to expire, and also in cases where the award may direct the delivery of the possession of lands, or that a party is entitled to lands, &c., then that the Court in Ontario—in Nova Scotia the Court or a Judge—may order the other party to deliver possession pursuant to the award, and such rule or order shall have the effect of a judgment in ejectment, and execution may issue, and sheriff deliver possession.

No such provisions exist in New Brunswick.

The 21st section of the Nova Scotia Act, like the 176th of the Ontario Act, provides that any agreement or submission in writing may be made a Rule of Court, unless in the agreement words purporting the negative appear. But the first section Nova Scotia does not, like the 179th Ontario, reiterate the exception, and leaves it, therefore, doubtful whether the Nova Scotia reference in that respect may not be capable of a different construction, namely, that in order that it may not be revocable, the agreement should contain those words, that the submission may be made a Rule of Court.

In Ontario, the costs of arbitrations are regulated by a Special Act. (29 Vic., chap. 32, 1865.)

In Nova Scotia, the arbitrators' fees are allowed at the discretion of the Judge, taxing the costs of the cause.

In New Brunswick, no provision is made relative thereto.

LANDLORD AND TENANT.

ONTARIO.	NEW BRUNSWICK.	NOVA SCOTIA.
Con. Stat. U.C., c. 27—303.	1 Vol. Rev. Stat., c. 126, p. 322, and 326.	Rev. Stat., c. 135, pages 140, 145, 586, 604, 613.
Con. Stat. U. C., c. 19—166.		
Stat. of 1860, c. 43, p. 92.	2 Vol. Rev. Stat., 12 Vic., c. 39, sec. 31 and 32, (Title Exor., and Admin., p. 359.	
Stat of 1867-8, p. 149.		
	Statutes of 1855, p. 91.	
	„ 1858, p. 75.	
	„ 1865, p. 67.	

LANDLORD AND TENANT.

Ejectment and the mode of Recovering Possession of Real Estate.

In *Ontario* the commencement of the proceedings to recover possession of real estate is simple and clear. The old English fictions of John Doe and Richard Roe and an imaginary tenancy are abandoned, and the first process is a writ directed to the person in possession by name, describing with reasonable certainty, the property claimed, and stating the names of all the persons in whom the title is alleged to be. To the writ a notice must be attached, stating the nature of the claimant's title, whether by grant, deed, or lease, &c., and from whom derived, according to the nature of the title, with reasonable certainty, and only one mode of title can be set up, unless leave of a Court or Judge be granted for more ; and at the trial the claimant is confined to the proof of the title alleged. This writ remains in force for three months, but must be returned within sixteen days after service, must be endorsed with the Attorney's or party's name like other writs, and is liable to the same proceedings for ascertaining the authority for issuing it, and who the claimants are, and their abode, &c., as on other writs. It may be served in the usual way, or in such mode as the Court or Judge may order ; and in case of vacant possession by posting copies upon door of dwelling-house or other conspicuous part of the property, it must issue from the proper office of the County in which the lands lie. Besides the original jurisdiction in the Superior Courts, jurisdiction in ejectment is under certain circumstances specified in the Act (23 Vic. chap. 42, Statutes of Canada), extended to the County Courts, when the yearly value of the premises or the rent, payable in respect thereof, does not exceed $200.

When judgment does not go by default, the party or parties named in the writ, may appear and defend for the whole or part as he or they may desire, specifying in the latter case the part with certainty ; and must file a notice not only denying claimant's title, but setting forth their own in the same manner as claimant is required to set forth his ; and in order to prevent mere intruders speculating on flaws in titles, the Plaintiff may give a notice, requiring Defendant to shew on the trial what legal right he has to the possession ; and on the trial mere formal defects are not allowed to prevail against the claimant if the Court and Jury are satisfied that in justice he is entitled to be regarded as proprietor, unless the Defendant shews that he is legally entitled, or that he *bona fide* claims to be legally entitled by reason of claimant's defective title ; or *bona fide* holds under the persons entitled. Judgment obtained under such circumstances cannot afterwards be used in evidence to entitle claimant to recover for *mesne profits*.

Provision is made for other persons than those named in the writ, to come in and defend by leave of a Court or Judge, and for the enforcing of judgments by executions, &c. ; and in case of joint tenants, or tenants in common, that an *actual ouster* must be proved before claiment can recover, and also that on the trial *mesne profits* may be allowed. A tenant served with a writ of ejectment forfeits three years' rack rent if he omits to notify his landlord ; and when the rent is six months in arrear, and landlord has power of re-entry, he may without formal demand or re-entry, serve a writ of ejectment and recover possession in case no sufficient distress was to be found upon the premises.

Tenants disputing may, under certain circumstances, be relieved in Equity on depositing in Court the arrears, costs, &c.

In the class of cases in ejectment coming within the County Court jurisdiction, an arrear of rent for sixty days with power of re-entry for non-payment, authorizes the writ.

In *Nova Scotia* the simple mode of proceeding as in Ontario also exists, but with the addition, that on the trial damages may be given for the Plaintiff, but there are none of those wise provisions operating against speculators in flaws in titles ; and the other provisions are not as full and explicit. The Defendant is not required to shew by what right he holds, or to set forth his title ; and formal defects in proof are not rendered inoperative. It is not stated that the damages shall be limited to *mesne profits*.

In *New Brunswick* the old English mode of proceeding in ejectment still prevails. John Doe and Richard Roe are in full force. To recover a city lot, the declaration which is served upon the party in possession describes it as ten lots—ten acres of wilderness land, ten acres of land covered with water, ten acres of arable land, ten acres of cultivated land, and ten acres of other land ; and John Doe by a notice at the bottom of the declaration gravely informs the party to whom the notice is addressed, that he John Doe has no claim to the lands above described, and that if he has any claim thereto, he had better appear in court and defend the same.

If the party to whom the notice is addressed sufficiently recognizes the description and does not permit judgment to go by default, he appears and the real description of the lot is subsequently set forth in a Consent Rule. On the trial the Plaintiff must make out his own case. If the proof of his deeds or their registration be defective, the defendant has nothing to do with it. He relies upon the position that possession is nine points of the law, and he is not called upon by the Court, or the practice to make any admissions. In other respects as to the rights of the Landlord to proceed in ejectment when rent is in arrear, and the relief of the tenant disputing, the provsions are substantially the same as in Ontario.

In both Ontario and Nova Scotia provision is made that in case a party defeated in ejectment afterwards brings another action for the same property, he may be compelled on an application to a Judge to give security for costs.

In *New Brunswick* no such provision is to be found, and the action for *mesne profits* is separate from the ejectment.

OVER-HOLDING TENANTS.

In *Ontario* under the Consolidated Statutes 313 (22 Vic. chap. 27), if a tenant refuses to go out after the expiration of his tenancy, the Landlord may in case he brings ejectment, by a notice require the tenant to find bail, if ordered by the Court or Judge for such damages as claimant may recover, and the Judge or the Court on summons and cause shewn, may order such bail, and on such conditions as deemed proper, and if party does not comply, judgment may be signed at once for the recovery of the possession.

There is a further provision under the 63rd and following sections of the same Statute, that the Landlord may, in case the tenant wrongfully refuses to go out, apply to the Court or Judge on affidavit, shewing that tenant wrongfully holds over without color of right, for a writ of inquisition in the Queen's name, which writ the Court or Judge is authorised to order to issue directed to a Commissioner appointed by the Court or Judge, commanding him to issue his precept to the Sheriff to summon a jury and try the question, notice of time and place being first served on tenant three days before, with copy of the affidavit and papers attached. The jury and witnesses are sworn, verdict taken, and writ with evidence returned by the Commissioner to the Clerk of the Crown and Pleas at Toronto ; and if the Court or a Judge at Chambers is satisfied that the case comes within the provisions of the 63rd section. Court or Judge may issue precept in the Queen's name to the Sheriff, commanding him forthwith to put landlord in possession.

The proceedings are open to revision, and if set aside, tenant restored, in order that question of right, if any, may be tried by ejectment.

By a later act passed by the Ontario Legislature in 1868, these latter powers are transferred to a County Judge, who may proceed without jury in a summary way the parties themselves being allowed to be witnesses (a provision which did not exist under former statute), and the proceedings are made part of the Records of the County Court. Such proceedings may be removed by *certiorari* to either of the Superior Courts of law, be set aside, and a writ of restitution issued and tenant restored in order that question of right may be tried in an action of ejectment,—proper powers are given for making rules, summoning witnesses, &c.

The powers created by the former Statute are not interfered with, and it is optional with the landlord under which he may proceed.

Monthly and weekly tenancies and notices to quit, and terms "Landlord" and "Tenant" defined, and forms added.

In *Nova Scotia*.—In case of tenants holding over after the expiration of the tenancy, and demand of possession, power is given to two Justices of the Peace, where lands lie, on complaint on oath, by warrant, to arrest party in possession, and detain him until he gives bail, to appear at the next term or sittings of Supreme Court in the County, to answer the complaint, and pay costs of the proceedings if adjudged against him. If security is not found, cause proceeds, and the proceedings before the Justices are filed in the Supreme Court.

Plaintiff's complaint, briefly stated, must be filed and served, and Defendant has fourteen days to file and serve notice of defence. The case is to be tried in a summary way, in the names of the parties, as a civil suit; if complaint is proved to satisfaction of the Court, writ of possession issues, executable within ten days, and treble the rent previously paid is to be allowed the landlord up to the time of his acquiring possession. But the Court, if it see fit, may order cause to be tried, and the rents or damages assessed by a Jury.

Notices to quit are regulated—yearly tenancies, three months; monthly tenancies, one month; weekly, one week.

Similar provisions, for recovery of possession, are given in cases of forcible entry and detainer, and in case of the former, for the awarding of damages; but no warrant is to issue in such cases when the Defendant, or the party under whom he claims, has been in quiet possession for the three years before the complaint.

In *New Brunswick*.—If a yearly tenant, or a person under, or in collusion with him, remains in posession, after notice to quit, determination of the tenancy, and demand of possession, landlord may recover double the rent or yearly value, in the same manner as any single rent may be recovered, the tenant may be held to bail, *and relief in equity is taken away*. In case of action brought against landlord, his Bailiff or Agent, for anything done under that Statute regulating landlord and tenant, he may plead general issue, and give special matter in evidence, and Plaintiff shall be liable to double costs.

When any tenant, after due notice and expiration of tenancy, refuses to deliver up possession, party entitled, may apply (on affidavit, stating facts, and designating premises) to two Justices of the Peace, where premises are situate, for summons, returnable in six days, to shew cause why he holds over, to be served with copy of affidavit on tenant, &c. If default be made, or no sufficient cause shewn, Justices, after hearing parties and evidence, may issue warrant to Sheriff to put landlord in possession, and to levy on goods and chattels of tenant for costs, and for want of goods and chattels, to render him to gaol of County for ———— days (specified in warrant).

In *Ontario*.—In case of an execution against the goods of a tenant, the right of the landlord, on proper notice to the officer having the execution, is preserved, to rent in arrear for one year, in cases of yearly tenancies; two terms, in cases of tenancies under a year; four weeks, in cases of weekly tenants, and is entitled to priority.

In *Nova Scotia and New Brunswick*.—The landlord's priority is preserved to one year's rent, irrespective of the extent of the tenancy, and the party executing the execution must pay such arrears before removing the goods.

DISTRESS FOR RENT.

In *Ontario* there are no Statutory provisions regulating the proceedings on distress for Rent. There is an Act (22 Vic., c. 123) respecting the costs of levying distress for small Rents and penalties.

In *New Brunswick and Nova Scotia.*—Distresses for Rent are regulated in detail by Statute.

In *New Brunswick.*—Goods seized for Rent, if not replevied within five days after distress and notice, are under the direction of the Sheriff or a Constable of the County, to be appraised by two sworn Appraisers, and after appraisement sold to the highest bidder ; they may be impounded on the premises, with free access to all persons connected with the distress.

Arrears may be distrained for, within six months after determination of the lease, if tenant's possession and landlord's interest, still continue.

Goods fraudulently or clandestinely removed from the premises to avoid distress, may be followed and distrained within thirty days, and sold *ut ante* (but no goods *bona fide* sold for valuable consideration before seizure, shall be distrained) and if such goods so fraudently or clandestinely removed are secured in a building or close, to prevent distress, the Sheriff must aid landlord to take, and if they be in a dwelling-house, on oath of reasonable suspicion made, may in day time break open same.

In case of rescue or pound breach, party injured may recover treble damages with costs against the offender, or against the owner of the goods distrained, if same come to his use or possession. Irregularity when Rent is justly due, does not make distrainer a trespasser, but party injured may recover damages, unless amends tendered before action brought.

In the case of goods liable to Rent, seized in execution, and the one year's arrears not paid, the officer must sell, pay the same, and apply residue to execution. The Queen's rights not be affected.

In *Nova Scotia* the proceedings are similar, except that in case of fraudulent removal, the time for following is twenty-four days ; in case of pound breach or rescue, the party aggrieved recovers his damages only (not treble damages) ; in the case of the one year's rent in arrear reserved on an execution for the Landlord, there is no provision for the Queen's rights, and there is no provision for the Sheriff breaking open door of a dwelling-house in cases of fraudulent removal.

There is provision made for distraining cocks of grain, or grain loose in the straw, &c., &c., and impounding same on premises, not to be removed therefrom to the damage of the owner, before sale ; and also for seizing cattle feeding upon any common, parcel of, or appurtenant to premises demised ; and for seizing growing corn, roots, fruits, &c., &c. ; and for cutting, gathering, curing, and laying them up, when ripe, on premises demised, and if no proper place therein, for removing them to some convenient place, and appraising and disposing of same towards Rents and charges,—appraisement not to be made until after crop cured or gathered, and notice of place of stowing served on tenant.

11

ARREST AND IMPRISONMENT FOR DEBT.

ONTARIO.	NEW BRUNSWICK.	NOVA SCOTIA.
Con. Stat. U.C., c. 24, p. 276.	2 Vol. Rev. Stat., page 353.	Rev. Stat., c. 134—516.
	1 Vol. Rev. Stat., Jurisdiction J. P., chap. 137.	Rev. Stat., Jurisdiction J.P., c. 128—466.
	Schedule of 1870.	

ARREST AND IMPRISONMENT FOR DEBT.

(Con. Stat. U. C. chap. 24, 276.)

In *Ontario*, no person can be arrested or imprisoned on *mene process* for debt, unless the cause of action amounts to $100, and an order has first been obtained from a Judge of a Superior or County Court, on affidavit, shewing facts to the satisfaction of the Judge, that there is probable cause for believing that such person, unless apprehended, is about to quit Canada with intent to defraud his creditors generally, or the plaintiff in particular. The Judge's order must specify the *time* within which, and the sum for which the party may be held to bail. Concurrent writs of *Capias* may then be issued, and the Judge, or the Judge of any County Court may grant the order for bail, though the process is intended to be issued, or an action has been commenced in either of the Superior Courts, as well as in his own Court. It is not necessary that at the time the affidavit was made it should be entitled in any Court; but the title of the Court may be added to the affidavit at the time of suing out the process, and shall thereafter for all purposes, civil or criminal, be considered as part of the affidavit *ab initio*.

The same power of arrest—under the same limitations—is extended to the Court of Chancery, and is then called a "Writ of Arrest," and is applicable in cases of alimony and *ne exeat*, but in the case of the Writ of Arrest, the bail is, not that the party will not go out of Canada, but simply that he will obey the orders made in the suit, and in case of being ordered into close custody, will render himself to the Sheriff accordingly. (22 Vic., chap. 24.) None of these provisions extend to persons who by law are privileged from arrest.

In *Nova Scotia* the power of arrest on *mesne process* is given on nearly similar conditions, but the amount need only be $20, and the Judge is to require nothing but the statement of the belief of the deponent, that debtor is about to quit the Province (not as in Ontario the grounds for the belief), and that he fears the debt will be lost if debtor is not arrested; the debtor on negativing on affidavit the fact of his being about to leave, if uncontradicted on the part of the plaintiff, may be discharged from custody, in the discretion of the Judge, with or without costs.

The arrest must be within one month after the date of the *Capias*. (Chap. 134, sec. 36, Rev. Stat. 516.)

In New Brunswick, the power of arrest for debt on *mesne process* is pure and simple. The plaintiff makes oath before any Commissioner for taking affidavits, that 2 vol. Rev. Stat. 353. defendant owes him. The sum must amount to $20, and thereupon the Attorney, who is also a Commissioner, takes the affidavit, issues the Writ, and defendant must pay, give bail, or go to gaol. It is not necessary to trouble a Judge, or make any inquiries, or to state whether defendant intends to stay in or leave the Province. The plaintiff swears he owes him, and that is sufficient. If defendant cannot get bail, he must stay in gaol, until discharged as an insolvent, or otherwise, by due process of law. In this respect, New Brunswick is far behind the other Provinces.

In the Magistrate's Court in New Brunswick, the power to arrest is given for sums from $2 to any sum under $20, and in Nova Scotia, from $4 to $20. In *New Brunswick*, by an act passed at the last session 1870, imprisonment in civil suits is limited to two years' actual confinement in gaol. The act is only for one year.

In Ontario, when the proceedings have been such that the defendant was held to bail on *mesne process*, he may be arrested on *Ca. Sa.* as a matter of course;—and in cases where he has not on special cause shown to a Judge, such as is required in the first instance, or that the defendant has made some secret and fraudulent conveyance of his property to prevent its being taken in execution, such Judge, may by a special order, direct a *Ca. Sa.* to be issued, and such writ may then be issued according to the practice of the Courts.

Process of arrest for contempt of Court on non-payment of monies ordered by the Courts of Chancery, Queen's Bench, Common Pleas, County Courts, or the Judges thereof, is abolished ; but in such cases, on such proof as would authorize the issuing of a *Ca. Sa.*, a writ of attachment corresponding to a *Ca. Sa.*, may, by special order, be obtained, and the order of the Court, directing the payment, is to be treated as a judgment, and the parties thereunto, are to be regarded as debtors and creditors, and entitled to like remedies as in corresponding Laws under the Act.

In *Nova Scotia* and *New Brunswick*, there is no special statutory provision authorizing an arrest on a *Ca. Sa.* for debt. The right to issue such an execution follows as an incident of the judgment which must have been obtained, and it is constantly put in force in both of those Provinces.

In all *three Provinces*, provisions exist and are made for giving the limits of the gaol to debtors imprisoned on *mesne* or final process, and for their discharge from imprisonment on either *mesne* or final process in case of delay or irregularity in his proceedings by the plaintiff, or the insolvency of the defendant.

In *Ontario*, it is enacted, no married woman shall be arrested on *mesne* or final process. In *Nova Scotia* and *New Brunswick*, no such provision is made, that being left to the Common Law where a married woman can be no party to a contract, the debt consequently being her husband's. No decision has yet been given how far her position in this respect may be altered in those two Provinces by the Statutes giving them separate rights and remedies from their husbands. The express enactment in Ontario would leave no question open.

In Nova Scotia and New Brunswick, it is enacted, that no female or minor shall be arrested on a *Capias* issued by a Justice. (N. S. 467, N. B. 365.)

There is no provision in either of the three Provinces against the arrest of a *femme-sole* of full age and indebted.

SEAMEN.

NEW BRUNSWICK.	NOVA SCOTIA.	ONTARIO.
1 Vol. Rev. Stat., c. 86–216.	Rev. Stat. cap. 75—282.	Con. Stat. Can., c. 43—550.
Cap. 87—219.	Stat. of 1865, c. 5.	(Quebec.)
	Stat. of 1869, c. 11.	

SEAMEN.

In New Brunswick, Seamen are privileged from arrest for debt incurred without allowance of Master of ship to which he belongs, while vessel within the Province, until after voyage performed, or he be discharged ; and in case of arrest he is to be immediately released, by any Judge of the Court from which the process issued, and, if amount be two pounds, or under, by any Justice of the Peace.

In Nova Scotia, no debt over $1, incurred by any Seaman after signing articles, can be recovered until the conclusion of the voyage.

In New Brunswick, a Seaman's property, under £20, cannot be detained by any person, and provisions are made for application to a Justice of Peace for redress. No person is allowed a lien thereon if, at the time of the application, it shall appear that the Seaman was a deserter.

In Nova Scotia, the restriction is limited to the keeper of a public house, and there is no limitation as to value ; provisions for redress substantially the same.

In New Brunswick, if a Seaman refuses to do duty, or absents himself without leave, complaint may be made by owners, consignee, or master, to any Justice of the Peace, and he may be arrested, and, on conviction, kept until delivered over to proceed on the voyage, the expenses to be paid by and recoverable from the complainant and to be deducted by him from seaman's wages.

In Nova Scotia, the complaint may be made by owner, Master, or Mate, and on conviction the Seaman may be sentenced to 30 day's hard labor in gaol, but if he consents to go on board his ship, he is to be sent, if the Master so request, the expenses, not exceeding $8, to be deducted from his future wages.

In New Brunswick, any person knowingly harboring a seaman deserter from his ship, on conviction before two Magistrates where the offence is committed, is liable to a penalty not exceeding £10—one-half to prosecutor, the other half to County Treasurer—and if, during a voyage, Seaman deserts, he also forfeits all wages coming to him from the vessel he has joined, to be detained by Master or owner of such vessel for the owner of the ship from which he deserted.

In Nova Scotia a Seaman deserter forfeits all his effects on board and wages due him, provided the circumstances of the desertion are entered in the log-book, duly certified by Master, mate, &c., or credible witness. Desertion is defined to be absence for 24 hours before sailing, without leave, or any circumstances showing intention not to return. Any one knowingly harboring any deserter, who shall have signed articles, or having reason to suspect him of being absent without leave, was liable to a penalty of $4, but it is now increased to $40, by amendment of Act of 1865, chap. 5—one-half to prosecutor, the other half to County.

In New Brunswick, search-warrants may be obtained on complaint before a Justice of the Peace, on oath by owner, consignee, or Master, to search any alleged suspected ship within any harbor of the Province, or any house or place within the County of the Justice of Peace, and if Seamen be there found, to be taken and dealt with by the Justice of Peace, by being sent on board, or committed until vessel is ready for sea.

In Nova Scotia there is no such provision.

In New Brunswick, contracts made for procuring Seamen for any vessel, declared void, and money paid for such purpose, recoverable back.

In Nova Scotia.—No such provision.

In New Brunswick and Nova Scotia.—Seamen only bound when articles have been signed.

In New Brunswick.—Any one aiding a Seaman to desert, liable to a penalty not exceeding £10.

In Nova Scotia.—No provision of that character.

In both New Brunswick and Nova Scotia.—Entering H. M. Naval Service is not desertion.

By the Nova Scotia Act, coasting vessels are exempt from its provisions.

The New Brunswick Act makes no such exemption.

In New Brunswick Seaman's wages, under £20, are recoverable before a Justice of Peace. In Nova Scotia, before two Justices and failing proceeds on recovery ;—in both Provinces vessel made responsible ; in cases of proceeding otherwise, than as in such case provided, in both Provinces plaintiff loses costs.

In the Nova Scotia Act are many excellent provisions, which are not found in the New Brunswick Act, such as examination of Masters and Mates of certain vessels—provisions for Board of Examiners—medicines on board—in case of sale of ship when abroad—discharge of men abroad—application for relief of destitute Seamen—payment of wages to Seamen, notwithstanding assignment or attachment, or incumbrances made by him—for certificates on discharge, &c.

In New Brunswick there is a Local Act, establishing a shipping office, and regulating the shipping of Seamen at the port of St. John, the provisions of which, on special application, may be extended by the Local Government to other ports in the Provinces, otherwise they are not affected. Coasting vessels are exempt from the St. John Act.

The Consolidated Statutes of Canada, chap. 43, make provisions, affecting the port of Quebec, but there does not appear any statute regulating Seamen in Ontario.

In Nova Scotia, since the amended Statutes of 1865, chap 5, the Law is the same as in New Brunswick, by 1st vol. Revd. Stats., 218, sect 7, namely : "If any person shall Sec. 2. " aid or entice any Seaman to desert from any such vessel, or provide him the " means of deserting therefrom, or, with that object, aid him in the removal of his chest, " bedding, apparel, or other property, from on board any such vessel, or convey him there- " from without the sanction of the Master, the person so offending shall, upon conviction, " be liable to the same penalties and forfeitures as contained in the last section."

12

STATUTE OF LIMITATIONS.

Personal Actions.

ONTARIO.	NEW BRUNSWICK.	NOVA SCOTIA.
Con. Stat., c. 9—31,'44-450.	1 Vol. Rev. Stat,, c. 140-408.	Rev. Stat. c. 154—641.
Con. Stat. U.C., c. 78—806.		Stat. of 1866, c. 12, p. 97.
Stat. of 1862, c. 20.		Do., p. 37.
Stat. of 1863, c. 45.		Stat. of 1865, Rev. Stat. 887.

STATUTE OF LIMITATIONS.

Personal Actions.

The statute of limitations as to Personal Actions, is, with some slight difference, the same in the three Provinces.

In New Brunswick and Nova Scotia, by specific re-enatment. In Ontario, partially by re-enactment, and partially by reference, under the Act respecting Civil Rights and Property, to the Statutes of 21st James 1st, chap. 16, and 4th and 5th Anne, c. 16.

But there exists in Ontario (chap. 20, Stats. of 1862, "Act relating to limitation of "actions and suits in Upper Canada,") a provision that, in all proceedings after 1st of July, 1869, a person who has been, or is resident out of, or absent from Upper Canada, shall have no longer period to commence or prosecute an action or suit, by reason of such non-residence, than if he had been resident, and all distinction in favor of non residents, or absentees, in reference to the limitation of actions is abolished. This applies to both Real and Personal Actions.

There was not only no provision of this nature in the other two Provinces, but it was directly contrary to the provisions in Nova Scotia up to 1865 ; and in New Brunswick, at the present time.

The distinction in personal actions is still kept up in New Brunswick, and was in Nova Scotia to 1865, as to all persons out of those two Provinces, who were therein allowed the like period after the removal of the disability arising from absence for bringing their actions which they would be allowed in ordinary cases.

In *Nova Scotia*, up to 1865, when an action was brought "to recover a balance "upon a mutual open and current account, where there have been reciprocal demands," the Statute would run from the time of the last item in the account claimed, or proved to be chargeable on the other side. (Sect. 7, chap 154.)

In *Ontario*.—By chap. 45, 1863, sect. 5, "Act to amend Laws of Upper Canada "affecting trade and commerce," it is declared "That no claim in respect of a matter which "arose more than six years before the commencement of such action or suit, shall be "enforceable by action or suit, by reason only of some other matters of claim comprised "in the same account, having arisen within six years next before the commencement of "such action or suit,"

In *New Brunswick* there are no Statutory provisions on these points.

In *Nova Scotia*, in 1865, by an Act passed, chap. 10, under the title, "*An Act to "amend the Laws affecting trade and commerce*," the Law in Nova Scotia has been changed, and assimilated to that of Ontario, both with regard to persons absent from the Province, and with reference to the statute of limitations running from the last item of an open account, only that upon the first point the similarity to Ontario is limited to personal actions only.

"The Law as it was in Nova Scotia, by chap. 154, Revised Statutes, section 9, "was, 'Actions by or against minors, married women, persons insane, imprisoned or out of

Sect 9.

"' the Province, may be commenced within the like period after the "' removal of the disability, as is allowed for bringing the action in "' ordinary cases.' "

But by chap. 10 of the Acts amending Statutes entitled "An Act relating to *trade "and commerce*," sec. 7, it is enacted, "No person or persons who shall be entitled to any "action or suit, with respect to which the period of limitation, within

Sect. 7.

"which the same shall be brought, is fixed by sect. 9 of chap. 154, of the "Revised Statutes (3rd series), shall be entitled to any time within which to commence, "and sue such action or suit beyond the period so fixed for the same, by reason only of "such person, or some one or more of such persons, being at the time of such cause of "such action or suit accrued out of the Province, or in the cases in which, by virtue of "the aforesaid section, imprisonment is now a disability, by reason of such person, or

" some one or more of such persons being imprisoned at the time of such cause of " action or suit accrued."

" Where such cause of action or suit, with respect to which the period of limitation " is fixed, by the aforesaid chap. 154, lies against two or more joint debtors, the person or " persons who shall be entitled to the same shall not be entitled to any time within which to " commence and sue any such action or suit against any one or more of such joint debtors, " who shall not be out of the Province at the time such cause of action or suit accrued, " by reason only that some other one or more of such joint debtors was or were at the " time such cause of action accrued, out of the Province ; and such person or persons so " entitled, as aforesaid, shall not be barred from commencing and sueing any action or " suit against the joint debtor or joint debtors, who was or were out of the Province at " the time the cause of action or suit accrued, after his or their return into the Province, " by reason only that judgment was already recovered against any one or more of such " joint debtors who was not or were not out of the Province at the time aforesaid."

" All actions of account, or for not according, and suits for such accounts as concern " the trade of merchandize between merchant and merchant, their factors or servants, shall " be commenced and sued within six years after the cause of such actions or

Sect. 6.   " suits ; or when such cause has already arisen, then within six years after " the passing of this Act ; and no claim in respect of a matter which arose more than six " years before the commencement of such action or suit, shall be enforceable by action or " suit, by reason only of some other matter of claim comprised in the same account having " arisen within six years next before the commencement of such action or suit.

STATUTE OF LIMITATIONS.

Real Estate.

ONTARIO.	NEW BRUNSWICK.	NOVA SCOTIA.
Con. Stat. U. C., c. 88, p. 868—873.	1 Vol. Rev. Stat., c. 139–398.	Stat. of 1866, c. 12, **33**.
Stat. of 1862, c. 20.		
Stat. of 1864, c. 210.		

STATUTE OF LIMITATIONS.

Real Estate.

The statutes of limitations as to real estate, in New Brunswick and Ontario, are in the main very much the same.

The following are the most striking differences :—

In *Ontario* there is no statutory limitation against the Crown.

In *New Brunswick* the Crown is barred after sixty years.

In *Ontario*, where the grantee of Crown lands has not actually settled the same, and possession has been taken by a trespasser when in a state of nature, the Statute of Limitations as between such grantee and the trespasser will only run from the time of knowledge of that fact by the grantee or his representatives. Sect. 3.

In *New Brunswick* there is no provision of this nature.

In *Ontario*, the possession of a younger brother is not to be deemed the possession of the heir. Sect. 14.

In *New Brunswick* there is no such clause.

In *New Brunswick*, when there has been no acknowledgment, but possession has not been adverse to the right or title of the party claiming, then such person, or the person claiming through him, may, notwithstanding twenty years shall have expired, make his entry or bring his action within five years next after the twenty. Sect. 15.

In *Ontario*, no such provision.

In *New Brunswick* it is enacted that no part of the United States or British North America, shall be considered "beyond seas" under the Act. Sect. 19.

In *Ontario* no such limited provision, but by c. 20, 1862, privilege from non-residence is abolished.

In *New Brunswick* a mortgagee may bring his action within twenty years after the last payment by the mortgagor, although more than twenty years have elapsed since the right of entry accrued (provided that such payment was made within twenty years after right of entry accrued).

In *Ontario* the mortgagee has the same right, but not qualified by the proviso.

In *Ontario*, provisions are made relative to estates tail.

In *New Brunswick*, estates tail having been abolished, no provisions are made relative thereto.

In *Ontario*, provisions are made with reference to easements.

In *New Brunswick*, none.

In *Ontario*, no arrears of rent or interest, in respect of any money chargeable on land, or any legacy, or any damages in respect of such arrears or interest, can be recovered beyond six years after the same may be due, or after an acknowledgment thereof in writing. Sect. 19.

In *New Brunswick*, there is no such provision, and the matter would be governed by the nature of the contract, whether parol or otherwise.

In *Ontario*, sect. 19, is qualified in favor of a subsequent mortgagee, who may, notwithstanding such section, recover arrears of interest during all the time a prior mortgagee has been in possession, even beyond the six years, if such prior mortgagee has been in possession one year before action brought.

In *New Brunswick*, there is no such provision.

In *Nova Scotia*, the Statutes, with reference to limitations in real and personal actions, were comprised in one chapter, 154, Revised Statutes, 3rd series, page 641 ; and the provisions, with regard to real estate, were extremely short.

But in a later Act, passed in 1866, the provisions with reference to real estate, have been extended, and made substantially the same as in Ontario and New Brunswick,—except that where in Ontario, all distinction with reference to residence or non-residence, or absence from the province, wherever it may be, relative to the time within which actions may be brought, is abolished, and in New Brunswick, for the same purpose, and to the same extent, the United States and British North America are declared not to be " beyond seas," in Nova Scotia, the distinction is preserved, and absence from Nova Scotia gives an additional ten years after return.

In *Nova Scotia*, the same clause is found as in Ontario, with reference to the limitation of six years, for the recovery of arrears of rent, but by a subsequent section, action for rent upon an indenture of demise may be brought within twenty years.

The latter is the law in New Brunswick, and it is probable that the construction of the 19th section, in Ontario, has been limited to parol contracts for rents.

The statutory provisions, with reference to easements in Nova Scotia are the same as in Ontario. But with reference to light, the City of Halifax is specially exempted from the application of the principle, that twenty years user, or enjoyment, gives a right to light.

WITNESSES ABROAD, EXAMINATION OF.

ONTARIO.	NEW BRUNSWICK.	NOVA SCOTIA.
Con. Stat. U. C., c. 32—405.	2 Vol. Rev. Stat., c. 34–335.	Rev. Stat., c. 135—570.

EXAMINATION OF WITNESSES ABROAD.

The provisions for this purpose in the three Provinces are the same, except that in *New Brunswick*, the Act of the Commissioners, in taking the evidence is not required as in Ontario, to be verified by affidavit, sworn before the Mayor or Chief Magistrate of the place where the Commission was executed. The maxim *"Omnia presumuntur rite,"* &c., being held applicable to the Commissioners, who are for the purpose regarded as officers of the Court, having been appointed under its seal.

And further that in *New Brunswick* before the Commission can be opened, or the evidence thereunder received on the trial of any cause, it must be proved to the satisfaction of the Judge trying the cause, that the witnesses examined are out of the Province or dead, or of unsound mind, &c., &c., or unable from other causes to attend, &c.

In *Ontario*, on the contrary, the Commission will be opened and the evidence received, unless the party objecting, shews that the Commission was not properly taken, or that the witness is of sound mind, and living within the jurisdiction of the Court at the time the examination is offered in evidence to the Court.

In *Nova Scotia* the Statute makes no particular direction as to the mode in which the Commission shall be executed or verified. The Court, or Judges, or Prothonotary, specifying any restrictions they deem necessary in the order granting the Commission, and the Commission when returned may be opened by the Prothonotary at the instance of either party, on notice given to the other party of the Commission being returned, and no objections to the examinations being read, will avail unless taken within eight days after such notice. The objections to be specified in writing, and their validity determined by the Court, or a Judge on summons.

MORTGAGES, SALES OF LANDS UNDER FORECLOSURE.

Nova Scotia.	New Brunswick.	Ontario.
Rev. Stat. c. 114—403. „ c. 124—435. „ 433.	2 Vol. Rev. Stat., c. 5—96.	Con. Stat. U. C., c. 12—57.

MORTGAGES.

Sale of Lands under Foreclosure of.

In *Nova Scotia* the Sale of Lands under foreclosure of Mortgages and the redemption thereof, are made the subject of provisions differing from the proceedings of the other Provinces for that purpose, and in the Act of 1866, 29 Vic., chap. 11, which restores exclusively to the Equity Court many matters that had been previously brought by the Acts amalgamating the Courts of Equity and the Courts of Common Law, within the cognizance of the latter, Chap. 114 of the Revised Statutes, 403, "Of the Sale of Lands under the foreclosure of Mortgages," is specially excepted, and it is declared that the proceedings thereunder, are to continue to be in the Supreme Court and before the Judges thereof.

In actions of ejectment, brought by a mortgagee or on bonds or notes secured by mortgage, or on any covenant in a mortgage, when no other suit touching the same matter is pending in the Court, the person entitled to the Equity of Redemption, may appear as Defendant, pay to the Plaintiff, or bring into Court the amount due, with costs, and thereupon the Court, by a rule, may compel the Plaintiff to re-convey to such Defendant, the land mortgaged, and deliver up all writings in his custody relating thereto. Provisions are made for service of the ejectment, in case one of the Mortgagors, should be an absent or absconding debtor; and further for notice on any persons who would have to be made Defendants, if the proceedings were in Chancery.

The Court may, if the amount due with costs is not paid, order the lands, after thirty days' advertisement by handbills in the County, to be sold at public auction by the Sheriff.

In case the Defendant is an absent or absconding debtor, he is entitled to a re-hearing at any time within three years after judgment, and plaintiff, when he obtains his rule for a sale, must give security for repayment, if judgment should be reversed on re-hearing. The deed is to be executed by the Sheriff, and the Court may award a writ of possession.

The Sheriff pays out of the proceeds of the sale, the debt to the Plaintiff, and the balance to any person the Court may direct, and the Court, with reference to such suits, and the equitable adjustment of the rights of all parties, is clothed with the same powers as the Court of Chancery.

In *Ontario and New Brunswick* there are no such statutory provisions, and the foreclosure and sale of lands under Mortgages (when no power of sale is given in the Mortgage), and the redemption thereof, have to be brought about by proceedings in the Court of Equity.

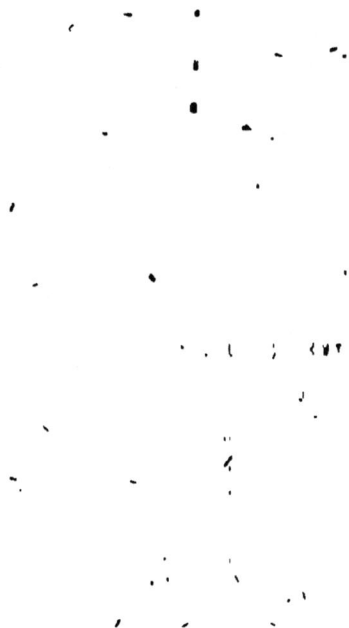

WITNESSES IN CIVIL CASES.

Parties to Cause.

ONTARIO.	NEW BRUNSWICK.	NOVA SCOTIA.
Con. Stat. U. C., c. 32—401.	Statute of 1856, c. 41.	Rev. Stat., c. 135—580.
Statutes of Ontario, 1867–8, cap. 1—56.		Stat. of 1865, page 13.
Statutes of Ontario, 1869, cap. 13, p. 31.		Stat. of 1867, cap. 19.
		Stat. of 1869, cap. 135.

WITNESSES AND EVIDENCE IN CIVIL CASES.

The law on this subject is, since the Act of the Ontario Legislature in 1869, the same in the three Provinces, with the exception of the difference pointed out in the case of executors or administrators, the representatives of deceased parties—the survivors, who may be parties to a suit not in such case being permitted in *Nova Scotia or Ontario* to give evidence on their own behalf, though compellable to do so on behalf of the opposite party.

ABSCONDING OR CONCEALED DEBTORS.

ONTARIO.	NEW BRUNSWICK.	NOVA SCOTIA.
Con. Stat. U. C., c. 25–286.	1 Vol. Rev. Stat., c. 125–315.	Rev. Stat., c. 141—605.
Con. Stat. U. C., c. 19–172.	Statutes of 1867, c. 10, p. 35.	Statutes of 1865.
	Statutes of 1859–65.	„ 1867.

ABSCONDING OR CONCEALED DEBTORS.

The essential difference between the three Provinces in this respect is, that in New Brunswick, the proceedings, when once taken against an absconding or concealed debtor, *enure* to the benefit of all the creditors of the debtor, whereas, in *Ontario* and *Nova Scotia*, they *enure* only to the benefit of such creditors as may have taken active steps to enforce their claims in that direction, and the Sheriff, who acts as trustee, only takes possession of so much property, as will meet with costs, the amount of the particular claims put in and proved on which the proceedings were taken.

In *New Brunswick*, on proceedings taken, the whole estate of the debtor, both real and personal, becomes by operation of law, vested in the trustees, who are afterwards to be appointed in accordance with the provisions of the Act relating to Absconding Debtors, and must (unless the proceedings are set aside by the return of the debtor, and he is acquitted of the act of absconding or concealment, for the purpose of defrauding his creditors, on due cause shown on personal examination and otherwise, before the Judge who issued the warrant) be divided among his creditors *pro rata*, according to law, at a general meeting, the surplus alone, if any, after full payment, being returned to the debtor, or his representatives.

In *Ontario*, before proceedings can be taken, the indebtedness must be to $100, and under certain circumstances in the Division Courts between $100 and $4.

In *New Brunswick* to $40.

In *Nova Scotia* to $20.

In *Ontario* and *New Brunswick*, the departure with intent to defraud, &c., must be verified by the oaths of two credible witnesses, in addition to the affidavit of the creditor or his agent, who applies for the attachment or warrant, of this fact, and the indebtedness.

In *Nova Scotia*, the affidavit of the creditor, or his agent (seeking the process or attachment) to that fact, and the indebtedness is sufficient without any verification.

In *Ontario*, the Writ of Attachment is issued in duplicate—contains a summons for personal service on the defendant, if he can be found, and is in force for six months. On receipt of the Attachment, the Sheriff is to seize all the absconding debtor's property as if on an execution, and with the aid of two freeholders, immediately to make an inventory thereof, and return the same with the Attachment.

In *Nova Scotia*, the creditor may proceed by summons, or attachment, or both. The Sheriff on the receipt of the Attachment, is to levy for the amount of the debt endorsed on the Writ, with $120, for probable costs in declaration causes, and $28 in summary causes, and the same is returnable within 20 days.

In *New Brunswick*, on the proof and verification required by the creditor to a Judge of the Supreme Court, or in his absence certain Commissioners provided for in the Act, and now by the County Court Act of 1867, a Judge of the County Court, a warrant is at once issued to the Sheriff, signed by the Judge or Commissioners, to seize all the Estate both real and personal of the debtor, make an inventory thereof, and return the same forthwith, the warrant to have the same priority as an execution.

The Judge who issues the warrant, at the same time orders a notice to be published in the *Gazette*, notifying all parties, that on the application of the creditor, he has ordered all the estate, real and personal of the debtor, to be seized; and unless he returns and discharges his debts within three months, such estate will be sold for payment thereof. The debtor is forthwith divested of all property, and all acts by him after such notice, and all payments of any debts, or delivery of any property to him, or to any persons but the trustees, afterwards to be appointed, are declared void. If the debtor does not return within three months and obtain a *supersedas* of the warrant, a Judge appoints three Trustees, who thereupon proceed to wind up the estate, and divide the proceeds, for which purpose they are vested with full legal powers.

In both *Nova Scotia* and *Ontario*, on the contrary, the proceedings are limited to the parties who inaugurated them ; and in both, the attachments are removed on the debtor putting in special bail in the proceedings.

In *New Brunswick*, provision is made that if the Sheriff takes any other party's goods by mistake, the claim of property is to be settled by a jury.

Provision, for the disposition of perishable property, made in all the provinces.

CORPORATIONS.

ONTARIO.	NEW BRUNSWICK.	NOVA SCOTIA.
Statutes of Canada, 1861, c. 18, p. 30.	1 Vol. Rev. Stat., c. 119.	Rev. Stat., c. 87—342.
Statutes of 1868, c. 1, p. 54.	Stat. of 1862, c. 86.	
Do. of 1867–8, c. 20, s. 46, p. 117.	Stat. of 1864, c. 44—107.	
	Stat. of 1867, c. 52.	
	Stat. of 1869, c. 72.	

CORPORATIONS.

The law *in Nova Scotia* on Corporations is embodied in one Act. Its provisions are simple and practical.

In *New Brunswick*, the law is also embodied in one chapter, except as to Mining and Manufacturing Corporations, the mode of sueing a Corporation, and of winding one up.

In *Ontario.*—Its main provisions are embodied in one Act, passed in 1861, entitled, " The Joint Stock Companies' General Clauses Consolidation Act."—(24 Vic., cap. 18.)

In both Provinces, *Ontario* and *Nova Scotia;* the law on this subject is in advance of the law of New Brunswick.

1st. In all three Provinces, shares and stock in such companies are for all purposes declared to be personal property.

2nd. In all three, contracts and acts of such companies done within the scope of their charters shall be valid, notwithstanding they may not be authenticated by the Corporate Seal.

3rd. In all three, such companies are vested with the requisite powers to make By-Laws, and to do all other legal acts necessary to accomplish the object of the Incorporation.

In *Nova Scotia* and *New Brunswick.*—Notwithstanding the expiration of the time for which they were Incorporated, or the termination of their charters by forfeiture, or otherwise; the Corporation is, nevertheless, continued for three years further, for the purpose of prosecuting and defending suits, settling and closing the concern, disposing of their property, and dividing their stock.

In *Nova Scotia,* there is a provision that the Real Estate of the Company may be sold, under execution, as Personal Estate.

There is no provision of this character in *New Brunswick* and *Ontario,* though, in both, as well as in *Nova Scotia,* the stock is made Personal Estate.

But the main difference is in the liability imposed upon the Directors in case of mismanagement of the affairs of the Company.

In Nova Scotia, the Directors of a company (the liability of whose members is limited by the Act of Incorporation) are made personally liable for any responsibility incurred by them on account of the Corporation, beyond the capital subscribed, unless the sanction of the company therefor be first obtained at a duly held meeting, held in accordance with the By-Laws, or the excess of dealing be specially authorised by the Act of Incorporation.

In *Ontario,* if the Directors declare and pay any dividend when the company is insolvent, or the payment of which makes the company insolvent, or diminishes the capital stock, they are made jointly and severally liable to the company, to the individual shareholders; and to the creditors thereof, for all debts of the company then existing, and for all that may be afterwards contracted during their continuance in office, respectively.

But any Director present at the time of the declaration of such dividend, or, if absent, within twenty-four hours after knowledge of the fact, and as soon as he is able to do so, may relieve himself of responsibility by entering his protest against such payment on the minutes, and within eight days thereafter publishing such protest in one newspaper near the place of business of the company—otherwise not.

Also, if any loan is made by the company to a shareholder, the Directors and officers of the company, making or assenting to the same, are made jointly liable to the company for the amount of the loan, and to third parties, to the extent of the loan with interest, for all debts of the company contracted from the time of the loan to the repayment.

They are also made jointly and severally liable on every contract of the company, when the words, "Limited," or " Limited Liability," are not written after the name of the company, where first occurring ; also, to all laborers, servants, and apprentices of the company for one year's wages, for services to the company performed while they are Directors, respectively.

But, that liability, under this section, 39th, is qualified :—

1stly. The company must be first sued therefor, within one year after the same became exigible.

2ndly. The Director must be sued therefor within one year thereafter.

3rdly. An execution against the company must first have been returned unsatisfied in whole or in part.

The liability of the Director will then be the amount due on the execution, with costs.

In *Nova Scotia*, unless the special Act creating the Corporation exempts its members from liability, each member is personally liable in his Real and Personal Estate for any debt due by the Corporation, in the same manner as if the same were his own private debt, in case an execution, on any judgment, against the Corporation shall be returned unsatisfied.—(Section 13.)

In *Ontario*, the liability of the shareholder is declared limited to the amount of the shares in the capital stock.—(Vide, clause 28, chap. 1, 1868, in addition.

In *New Brunswick*.—By an Act passed in 1862 (25 Vic., chap. 28), amended by an Act passed in 1869 (32 Vic. chap. 35), special provisions are made for Corporations for mining and manufacturing purposes, but there is no Act of the general character of *the Ontario and Nova Scotia Acts.*

In both *Nova Scotia* and *New Brunswick*, companies are specially interdicted from banking business, unless specially authorised, and also in Ontario by sect. 7, 28 clause, chap. 1, 1868, " Interpretation Act."

In *Ontario*, the major part of the Directors, after those first named in the special Act creating the company, must be residents of the Province (old Canada), and subjects of Her Majesty by birth or naturalization.

In *New Brunswick* and *Nova Scotia*, no such provision.

In *Nova Scotia*, special provisions are made with reference to arbitrations by companies, and to their annually filing in the Provincial Secretary's Office returns of their receipts and expenditures, profits and losses, and for the appointment of trustees to wind up the affairs of such companies on the expiration or forfeiture of the charters.

In *Ontario* and *New Brunswick*, no such special provisions are found, but in *New Brunswick* the winding up of the affairs of incorporated companies is done under a special Act for that purpose.—(27 Vic., chap. 44, 1864.

MARRIAGE, SOLEMNIZATION OF.

Ontario.	New Brunswick.	Nova Scotia.
Con. Stat. U. C., c. 72–787.	1 Vol. Rev. Stat., c. 106–269.	Rev. Stat., c. 120.
Stat. of 1861, c. 46.	Stat. of 1861, c. 9, p. 21.	Cap. 31, Statutes of 1865.
Stat. of 1868–9, c. 30.	Stat. of 1869, c. 17, p. 32.	„ 28, „ 1866. „ 18, „ 1867.
Stat. of 1869, c. 22, 33 Vic.	Stat. of 1870, p. 171.	„ 2, „ 1868.

MARRIAGE.

In *Ontario*, every minister and clergyman, duly ordained or appointed according to the rites of the church or denomination to which he belongs, and resident in Upper Canada, may, according to the rites thereof, solemnize marriage between any two legally qualified to contract marriage.

In *New Brunswick*, he must further be a British subject, not engaged in any secular calling, and have charge of a congregation in the Province, or be connected therewith, and be a Christian minister or teacher, duly ordained according to the rites of his denomination.

In *Nova Scotia*, any person recognized as a duly ordained minister by any congregation of Christians within the Province.

In *Ontario* and *New Brunswick*, exceptional provisions are made in favor of Quakers. In *Nova Scotia*, none.

In *New Brunswick*, the Governor in Council has power also to appoint certain Justices of the Peace to solemnize marriage ; and also on proof of one year's residence, and other compliances with the requisites before named, to authorize an alien minister to do the same ; notice of the granting of such licence must be published in the Royal Gazette, and it is revocable on cause.

The parties solemnizing the marriage are to transmit a certificate thereof to the Clerk of the Peace ; and in Ontario he is entitled to demand from the married couple therefor 25 cents, in New Brunswick, 50 cents.

Corresponding provisions for the issuing of marriage licences, for the registration of marriages, and the transmission of the statement thereof to the Government are made in all three Provinces.

BILLS OF EXCHANGE AND PROMISSORY NOTES.

ONTARIO.	NEW BRUNSWICK.	NOVA SCOTIA.
Con. Stat. U. C., c. 42–440.	1 Vol. Rev. Stat., 295.	Rev. Stat., 287.
Con. Stat. of Canada, cap. 57—681.	2 Vol. Rev. Stat., sec. 38–361.	Rev. Stat., cap. 82—**319.**
Statutes of 1864, c. 63.	Stat. of 1859, c. 22—76.	Rev. Stat., c. 134, sec. 270, page 354.
Statutes of 1865, c. 26.	Stat. of 1860, c. 31-48 & 9.	
	Stat. of 1867, c. 34—59.	

BILLS OF EXCHANGE AND PROMISSORY NOTES.

The damages on Protested Bills, &c., &c., differ in each Province.

In *Ontario*, if drawn on any person in Europe, or in the West Indies, or in any part of America not within any British American Colony, or the United States, 10 per cent. damages, 6 per cent. interest, and charges protest and postage.

If drawn on any person in any British North American Colony, or in the United States, 4 per cent. damages, interest and charges as before. (Consolidated Statutes of Upper Canada, cap. 43, page 442.)

If drawn on any person in Asia, Africa, Australia, New Zealand, Japan, Sandwich Islands, Mauritius, Madeira, or places not coming within the above definition, no provision made.

In *New Brunswick*, if drawn on a person and payable in *any part* of North America, without the Province, or in Prince Edward's Island, or Newfoundland, and protested, damages 2½ per cent., with legal interest (6 per cent.), and charges, &c.

If drawn on any person in and payable in Europe, the West Indies, or in any other place without the Province (other than as first recited), and protested, damages 5 per cent., with current rate of exchange and interest and charges.

In *Nova Scotia*, if drawn on any person in any part of North America without the Province of Nova Scotia, and protested, damages 5 per cent., interest 6 per cent. ; nothing about charges or postage.

If drawn on a person in any other country, damages 10 per cent., and interest 6 per cent.

Again, when the date of a note falling due comes on a public holiday or non-juridical day, a *dies non*.

In *Ontario*, it becomes due the day after the holiday.

In *New Brunswick*, the day before the holiday.

In *Nova Scotia*, no specific provision is made by statute, and therefore the English law would prevail, and the note would fall due on the day preceding—the 13th section of chapter 1 of the Construction of Statutes, providing " if the day in which an Act is to be " done falls on a Sunday, Christmas, or Good Friday, the same shall be performed on the " day following," must, it is presumed, be construed as having reference only to Acts required to be done by Statute.

In *Ontario*, there are many provisions for the recovery and regulation of proceedings on Bills of Exchange and Promissory Notes made Statutory, which in reality are only declaratory of the well-known law affecting Bills of Exchange and Promissory Notes, and as such are recognized and acted upon by the Courts in New Brunswick and Nova Scotia, and not hitherto deemed necessary in those Provinces to be specifically enacted.

In other respects the law is substantially the same.

MUNICIPALITIES.

NEW BRUNSWICK.	NOVA SCOTIA.	ONTARIO.
2 Vol. Rev. Stat., c. 8, p. 49.	Rev. Stat., c. 133.	Con. Stat. U. C., c. 51–151.
1 Vol. Rev. Stat., chapters 97, 42, 43, 44, and 45.		Con. Stat. U. C., c. 133.
Stat. of 1854, 18 Vic., c. 3.		
Statutes of 1856, 104.		
„ 1862, 104.		
„ 1865, 65.		
„ 1870, 122.		

16

·MUNICIPALITIES.

The powers of a Municipality, when once established, with reference to its control over local affairs, are in the several Provinces substantially the same ; though in Ontario, for the purpose of incurring debts, issuing debentures, and aiding and constructing Public Works, they are more extensive than in the other two Provinces—but the essential difference lies in the mode of their inception.

In *Ontario*, the inhabitants of every county or union of counties erected by proclamation into an independent county or union of counties, and of every township or union of townships erected into an independent township or union of townships, and of any locality erected into a city, town, or incorporated village, and of every county or township separated from any incorporated union of counties or townships, and of every county or township, or of the counties or townships, if more than one remaining of the union, after separation, being so erected or separated after the Act takes effect (1866), shall be a body corporate under the Act.

It is not a matter of option ; the law, under certain circumstances, creates the municipality, and the duties and responsibilities of such a Corporation thereupon follow as a matter of course.

In *Nova Scotia* and *New Brunswick*, it is optional with the inhabitants of a county whether they will be incorporated or not ; and in each Province, the mode by which that option shall be declared is specifically pointed out, viz. :—By public meetings in *New Brunswick*, called on a petition to the sheriff of at least one hundred of the resident freeholders or householders of the county paying rates upon property, praying for the calling of public meetings for such purpose. After one months' public notice of such meetings and the object, given by the Sheriff of the County, the meetings are held at each of the polling places in each parish, printed handbills, publishing the calling thereof and the object, in ten of the most public places in each parish, having first been printed and put up. At each meeting, the town or parish clerk or presiding officer returns the lists of the votes both for and against to the Sheriff, who adds the same up and declares the result, and if a majority of ratepayers on property (19 Vic., c. 37) vote for the incorporation, the Sheriff certifies the same to the Governor in Council, who thereupon grants a Charter.

(margin: 2 vol., Rev. Stat., c. 8. Repealed.)

(margin: 18 Vic., c. 4. 1855.)

In *Nova Scotia*, on a Petition by one hundred freeholders to the Sheriff, who shall thereupon name a day and place for simultaneously holding a public meeting in each Electoral District in the County, first giving, in each District in three of the most public places, ten day's notice thereof, by printed handbills, with a copy of the petition affixed, setting forth the object.

In *New Brunswick* and *Nova Scotia*, the right of incorporation is limited to counties, and does not extend to townships or subdivisions of counties as in *Ontario*.

The *Municipal Act of Ontario* is more elaborate, comprising 429 sections, and containing provision for almost every subject that may arise in the administration of the local affairs of a county or subdivison thereof.

In *New Brunswick* and *Nova Scotia*, the laws authorising municipalities have never been acted upon to the same extent that they have been in Ontario, and the local affairs of most of the counties, are still managed by the old system of Grand Juries, Sessions, and Justices of the Peace.

PARTITION.

ONTARIO.	NEW BRUNSWICK.	NOVA SCOTIA.
Stat. of 1869, c. 33—157.	2 Vol. Rev. Stat., c. 6—99.	Rev. Stat., c. 139—597.

PARTITION.

The partition of lands in *New Brunswick* falls under a branch of the Act relating to the administration of Justice in Equity.

In *Nova Scotia*, it falls under a division of the law relating to Real Property, whilst in *Ontario* it constitutes a distinct provision by itself, passed since Confederation, entitled: " An Act respecting the partition and sale of Real Estate in the Province of Ontario."

In *New Brunswick*, the proceedings have to be on the Equity side of the Supreme Court, somewhat according to the forms in Chancery.

In *Nova Scotia*, by proceedings in the Supreme Court of the County, and before a Judge at Chambers, in the same manner as in ordinary cases in that Court.

And in *Ontario*, in any of the Superior Courts of Law or Equity, when the lands lie in different Counties—when they lie in one County—before the same Courts, or a County Court in addition.

In *New Brunswick*, such compulsory partition is limited to co-partners, joint tenants, and tenants in common.

In *Nova Scotia*, the same, whilst in *Ontario*, in addition to those it embraces parties entitled to dower, tenants by the courtesy, mortgagees or other creditors having liens, and all parties whomsoever interested in the lands sought to be partitioned.

Assignment of Dower is regulated both in *New Brunswick* and *Nova Scotia* by separate Act, and in a different mode.

In *New Brunswick*, mortgagees and other persons holding liens, or interested in the lands, are not included in the law relating to partition; but are left to their ordinary legal rights and remedies, and subject to any provisions affecting them embraced in the Imperial Act of 13 & 14 Vict. cap. 60, introduced into New Brunswick in 1867.

In *Ontario* they may or may not be made a party to the proceedings at the option of the petitioner, and if not made a party, their lien shall not be affected.

In *Nova Scotia* any person interested in the premises as a mortgagee or otherwise, upon the share of any part owner, may appear and defend, whether named in the petition or not ; but whether he appears or not, he will be concluded by the Judgment so far as respects the partition and assignment of shares, but his lien upon the part owners' share will remain in force.

For making out the partition, after due hearing and order made by the Court, three Commissioners are appointed by the Court in *New Brunswick* and *Nova Scotia*.

In *Ontario*, for that purpose the Judge of the Surrogate Court in each County is made the real representative, and under the order of the Court, duly obtained, makes the partition.

Provision is made in each of the Provinces of *Ontario* and *New Brunswick* for sale of the land, in case an exact or minute partition would be prejudicial. In *Nova Scotia* provision is made for adjustment only—no sale.

In *Ontario* and *Nova Scotia* the details and modes of proceeding in general, and in exceptional cases, are pointed out at great length, while in *New Brunswick* they are left as in a great degree in most cases in Equity, to the review and supervision of the Court.

LUNATICS, ESTATES OF.

ONTARIO.	NEW BRUNSWICK.	NOVA SCOTIA.
Con. Stat. U. C., c. 12—52.	1 Vol. Rev. Stat., c. 88—222.	Rev. Stat., Lunatics.
Stat. of 1865, c. 17.	Stat. of 1869, c. 9.	
Stat. of 1865, c. 18.		

ESTATES OF LUNATICS.

In *Ontario* the control and management falls within the power and jurisdiction of the Court of Chancery to the same extent that it does in England, and will be found in the statute relating to that Court (chap. 12, 22nd Vic. con. Stat. U. C. 45).

The term Lunatic includes Idiots, and the Court has power on evidence to declare a party a lunatic without issuing a commission, except in cases of reasonable doubt. In the case of a commission, a period not exceeding six months was allowed to traverse, and the trial took place before any Court of Record, or a Judge of the Court of Chancery with a jury, or without a jury (chap. 17, 28 Vic. 1865).

By the latter Act the right of traverse is taken away, and in lieu thereof a new trial or new trials are granted under certain regulations, and on such enquiry the Lunatic must be produced, if within jurisdiction.

In *New Brunswick* a person must be found lunatic by a commission de *lunatico inquirendo*, which was formerly done by a commission in nature of a writ de *lunatico inquirendo* under the Great Seal, but is now (by an Act passed in 1869, c. 9) by application under oath, to a Judge of the Supreme Court who orders commission to issue under Seal of the Court, and the proceedings thereupon had are in accordance with the practice of, and by that Act, to be conducted in the *Court of Chancery.* (Memo.—No Court of Chancery there ; mistake in passing Act ; Equity side of Supreme Court.)

In *Nova Scotia* no commission is necessary. Application is made to Superior Court, or a Judge thereof by the friends of the insane person, or the overseers of the poor where he is an innabitant, to have a guardian appointed ; and the Court or Judge after 14 days notice, hears and dismisses, or appoints a guardian of his person and estate. The guardian has to give bonds, and his duties are clearly and succinctly defined.

In *Ontario* the management of the Estate, after the party has been found a lunatic, is vested in a Committee appointed by the Court, whose powers are also clearly defined, and by whom security has also to be given. The powers and duties of the Committee are substantially the same as those of the guardian in Nova Scotia.

In *New Brunswick* the management is by a Committee as in Ontario, and the duties though differently defined, are substantially the same. There is no specific provision that the Committee should give security ; but the requiring that would clearly come within the powers of the Court appointing, and is always required.

In *New Brunswick* the creditors, as well as the Committee, may apply to have the freehold and leasehold Estate, sold and encumbered to pay debts or perform contracts of the Lunatic, before lunacy.

LUNATIC ASYLUMS AND DANGEROUS LUNATICS.

ONTARIO.	NEW BRUNSWICK.	NOVA SCOTIA.
Con. Stat. U. C., c. 71-784.	1 Vol. Rev. Stat., c. 90—226.	Rev. Stat. c. 152—634.
	Do., c. 89—224.	
	Stat. of 1859, c. 30—84.	
	Stat. of 1869, c. 124.	
	Stat. of 1870, 41 & 42.	
	Dominion Act, 31 Vic., c. 40.	

LUNATICS.

Lunatic Asylums and Dangerous Lunatics.

The property in Provincial Lunatic Asylums, in the three several Provinces is vested in the Crown, but the management in each is different.

In *Ontario,* its financial and business affairs are managed by a Bursar, its medical and moral treatment by a medical Superintendent, both appointed by the Government, holding office during pleasure, and annually making their reports to the Government and Assembly, and the medical Superintendent in addition to the visiting inspectors. Salary of medical Superintendent not to exceed $2,000 ; Bursar, $1,200.

In *New Brunswick.*—The management is by not less than five, or more than nine commissioners, appointed by the Government, the senior commissioner being chairman ; three a quorum ; and the majority ruling—their powers extend to making regulations for management, conditions of admission, and discharge of patients, (subject to confirmation, disallowance, or amendment by Governor in Council), appointing servants, furnishing provisions, and enforcing regulations. A record of all proceedings to be kept, open at all times to the inspection of Governor in Council, and persons appointed by either branch of Legislature to examine, but no servant or officer to be appointed, unless at meeting, where at least five commissioners are present. No commissioner to receive compensation, or hold any office of emolument connected with Asylum, or be a contractor, or security for contractor, for, or on account of Asylum, or repairs to the Asylum, under the Board of Works.

In *Nova Scotia,* the financial and general management is in the Board of Works, subject to instructions or restraint by the Governor in Council.

The By-Laws are made by the Board of Works, subject to approval of Governor in Council, and the law of the land.

The Governor, the Chief Justice, Provincial Secretary, President of Legislative Council, and Speaker of House of Assembly, and the Heads, or authorised representatives of Christian churches in the Provinces, are *ex officio* visitors. The Governor appoints medical Superintendent, salary $2,000, without board or lodging ; Superintendent appoints his subordinates, and determines their salaries and wages, and is the chief executive officer, must be a well educated physician, and with his family reside on the premises, and devote his whole time to the institution.

In *Ontario,* a certificate of three medical men, verified and signed by principal municipal officer of the locality, setting forth a cotemporaneous and joint examination, is required for committal of Lunatic, and is a sufficient authority to any person to convey, and authorities at Asylum to detain Lunatic.

In *New Brunswick,* provisions of this nature are limited to dangerous Lunatics, who, on proof of the danger, may be apprehended on Warrant by two Justices, and committed to the Provincial Asylum.

In *Nova Scotia,* when Lunatic is dangerous, or suffering unnecessary distress or hardship, two Justices on application, to investigate, with assistance of one or more duly qualified medical practitioners, and, on proof of insanity, certified by such practitioner, or practitioners, in writing, the Sheriff or Justices to issue Warrant for apprehension, in case before apprehension, only one medical practitioner has certified, he must be examined by two, appointed by the commissioners, (?) before being admitted to Hospital.

In *Ontario,* provision is made for the payment to the Asylum of the cost of the maintenance of the Lunatic, if under 21 years of age, by his parents, guardian, or committee, if able to pay, and, in case of refusal or omission for the trial of that question, and, if he be possessed of Real or Personal Estate, and has no guardian or committee, the Bursar may, if property is more than sufficient to maintain the family of the Lunatic, take possession of so much as may be necessary to maintain him, and manage the same as such Lunatic might do if of sound mind, and legal age, but before any sale or conveyance of any Real Estate of Lunatic, the Bursar must obtain approval of the County Judge, and, n case of doubt as to right of property, may have an inquisition before the Connty Judge, and the Bursar is to be liable to account like any other trustee.

In *New Brunswick*, when the Lunatic is received into the Asylum as a boarder, a bond to the Queen has to be entered into by the person sending him, for his support, but, in case of being committed as a dangerous Lunatic, the expenses of his apprehension are to be paid in the first instance out of the contingent funds of the County, by order of the sessions, and are made recoverable by Warrant of distress by any two Justices, on any goods and chattels of the Lunatic, wherever found, for reimbursement of sessions, overplus, if any, being paid to commissioners of Asylum for his support, or to abide order of Court of Equity.

In *Nova Scotia.*—In the case of patients sent to the Asylum, the expense of maintenance, removal, or funeral expenses, may be recovered by the Board of Works, in the same manner as debts of a like nature, in case the guardians, or other parties liable, have omitted or refused to pay the same to the Receiver Generel on demand ; but, in the cae of pauper Lunatics, the expenses are chargeable and recoverable by assessment, or in case of omission to assess by amercement of the Supreme Court, on the respective Counties or Districts in which the Lunatics shall have obtained a legal settlement.

In *Nova Scotia*, dangerous Lunatics, apprehended for the prevention of crime, or acquitted on trial for any offence on the ground of insanity, may be committed to the Gaol of the County or Provincial Lunatic Asylum, as the Governor may see fit, and the expenses of the apprehension (paid in the first instance by Treasurer out of County funds) in case of want of Real or Personal Estate of Lunatic, out of which same may be realized, are made a charge against the County in which he had his last legal settlement, and for his maintenance in Gaol (until such time as he may be removed by order of Governor to the Lunatic Asylum), are recoverable by order of two Justices from the overseers of the Poor of the township, or place adjudged to be his legal settlement, and where no legal settlement can be ascertained, from the Treasurer of the County where he was apprehended, subject to appeal to next General or Special Sessions against such orders.

In *Ontario*, the provisions, with reference to criminal or dangerous Lunatics, are substantially the same as in Nova Scotia, except that in Ontario in cases of persons becoming insane, pending imprisonment, either under sentence, or under criminal charge—of the two Justices of the Peace, by whom the question of sanity is to be determined, one must be Chairman of the Quarter Sessions for the County, who is (by chap. 17, 22 Vic., sec. 5, Con. Stats. Upper Canada) Judge of the County Court.

The expenses of apprehension and maintenance, in the absence of goods and chattels, or annual rents of lands and tenements of the Lunatic, are made chargeable upon his place of settlement, which is, for the purposes of that Act, declared to be one year's residence, if of full age ; if a minor, by being married, and living separately from father's family ; if a female, living one year with her husband ; if an apprentice, serving one year, or being hired and earning one year's wages. No child born in any Hospital or Asylum thereby to gain a settlement.

INFANTS.

Ontario.	New Brunswick	Nova Scotia.
Con. Stat. U. C., c. 74–795.	1 Vol. Rev. Stat., c. 126–356.	Rev. Stat., s. 127—453.
Con. Stat. U. C., c. 12—56.	Do., c. 136, sec. 44.	121, sec. 2 & 5.
		124, p. 440.
	Do., c. 121, sec. 2 & 5.	
	Stat. of 1860, c. 3.	
	2 Vol. Rev. Stat., c. 4, p. 94.	

ILLEGITIMATE CHILDREN.

Ontario.	New Brunswick.	Nova Scotia.
Con. Stat. U. C., c. 77–805.	1 Vol. Rev. Stat., c. 57–137.	Rev. Stat., c. 91—357.
	Stat. of 1869, c. 36.	

INFANTS, GUARDIANSHIP.

As a general rule in all of the three Provinces, the Court of Chancery, or, as it is represented in New Brunswick and Nova Scotia by the equity side of the Supreme Court, has the ultimate control of the infants and their estates, and the appointment and removal of Guardians.

In *Ontario*, the primary appointment of a guardian, however, rests exclusively with the Surrogate Court for the county within which the infant resides, in cases where the infant has no father, or guardian-at-law, to take charge of the person and estate.

In *Nova Scotia*, the father of unmarried children under twenty-one years of age, may by instrument in writing, executed in presence of two witnesses, dispose of their custody and tuition, though the father himself be under twenty-one years of age. In case he does not, the power is with the Judge of Probates (on application by the minor, or some relative, or the executors or administrators of the estate) who must appoint the next of kin, unless on good cause shewn, he selects some other person ; but on attaining fourteen years of age, the infant may select his own guardian, which appointment is to be confirmed by the Judge of Probates, on the guardian nominated giving the requisite security.

In *New Brunswick*, when the estate does not exceed the value of £500, the Judge of Probates within his jurisdiction, on petition of the infant verified by affidavits, may appoint a guardian for the estate, who shall enter into recognizances faithfully to perform the duties of his office.

Where the estate is over £500, no statutory provision being made, the matter would fall within the control of the Supreme Court in Equity.

With reference to the management of the estates of infants, provisions substantially the same are made in all the Provinces.

APPRENTICES AND MINORS.

Ontario.	New Brunswick.	Nova Scotia.
Con. Stat. U. C., c. 19–145.	1 Vol. Rev. Stat., 347.	Rev. Stat.
Con. Stat. U. C., c. 76–801.	Statutes of 1868, c. 13.	

APPRENTICES AND MINORS.

In *Ontario* and *New Brunswick*, the same power is given to a minor to sue for wages, in the former, in the Division Court to $100, in the latter, to $200 in the County Court.

In *Nova Scotia* there is no such provision.

But in *Ontario* a minor over 16 years of age, who has no parent or guardian, is virtually made of age, and may sue and *be sued* on his contract.

Not so in *New Brunswick* or *Nova Scotia*. In these Provinces while a contract to his benefit may be enforced by him, he himself cannot be sued upon his contract, and in enforcing his contract for himself, he would have to sue by *prochain ami* or guardian *ad litem*. Except in New Brunswick in the case of "wages due to him," when by 31st Vic., c. 13, A.D., 1868—in amendment of the County Court Act—he is made *quoad* the recovery thereof of full age.

Under 14—in both *Nova Scotia* and *New Brunswick*, minors may be bound as apprentices until 14 years of age, by parent or guardian without consent—above 14 years of age, with consent; but in both cases must be by indenture in two parts, one part kept by the parent, or Clerk of the Peace for the minor.

In *Ontario*, at 14 years of age, similar provision as to consent required ; but in case of abandonment of infant child by father, the mother may with approbation of two Justices, before 14 years of age, bind male child until 21 years of age, female until 18.

In all three Provinces, the Local Authorities have power to bind children chargeable.

In *Ontario*, the consent of the minor is required.

In *New Brunswick*, he is to be examined as to whether he has any just objection, and the Justice of the Peace must give certificate to that effect, or indenture will be void.

In *Nova Scotia*, there is no such qualifying clause.

In *Ontario*, provisions for punishing apprentices for disobedience or improper conduct are given to any Justice, Mayor, or Police Magistrate, and extend to commitment to House of Correction for three months.

In *New Brunswick*, the power is given to two Justices of the Peace, and extends to one month only to the Common Gaol.

In *Ontario*, complaints by apprentices against masters, heard before one Justice of Peace, &c., &c., and punishment by fine not exceeding $20.

In *New Brunswick*, heard before two Justices of Peace, who may order discharge or other relief to apprentice.

In *Nova Scotia*, same as in New Brunswick.

In *Ontario*, in case of the death of the master, apprentice by operation of law is transferred to person who continues the establishment of deceased, and master has powers to transfer apprentices to any person carrying on same business, who is competent to take apprentices.

In *New Brunswick*, master has no power to assign or transfer apprentices, and death puts an end to the contract.

In *Nova Scotia*, the statute is silent on this point.

In *Ontario*, the duties of the master towards apprentice are defined by statute, section 7.

In *New Brunswick*, and *Nova Scotia* they are required to be set out in the indenture.

In *Ontario*, the duties of the apprentice are defined.

In *New Brunswick*, and *Nova Scotia*, not.

In *Ontario*, proceedings against absconding apprentices are limited to three years.

In *New Brunswick* and *Nova Scotia*, no such provisions, therefore governed by ordinary law.

In *Ontario* and *New Brunswick* there are penalties for harboring indented apprentices. In Nova Scotia, none.

In *Ontario*, provisions are made for avoiding the indentures, if apprentice becomes insane, or is convicted of felony.

In *New Brunswick* and *Nova Scotia*, there are no such provisions.

In *New Brunswick*, no sale on credit to apprentice allowed, and in actions thereon declared void. Masters of vessels harboring apprentices liable to £10 penalty.

Every master ship builder is bound to have two apprentices for four years each, and forfeits £50 for every vessel of 150 tons or upwards he builds, without having any such apprentices.

In *Nova Scotia* and *New Brunswick*, a special section of the act authorises parents and guardians and persons who bind out minors to enquire into their treatment, and defend them in case of ill-treatment or misconduct by their masters.

In *Ontario*, there are no special provisions of this character.

AFFIDAVITS AND AFFIRMATIONS MADE ABROAD.

ONTARIO.	NEW BRUNSWICK.	NOVA SCOTIA.
Stat. of 1863, c. 41—107.	Stat. of 1864, c. 40—90.	Rev. Stat., c. 144—672.
	Stat. of 1856, c. 41—113.	„ c. 135—577.
	Stat. of 1860, c. 26.	
	Stat. of 1862, c. 31.	

AFFIDAVITS, AFFIRMATION, &c., ABROAD.

The Acts of *Ontario* and *New Brunswick* on this subject are the same, except a clause in one of the New Brunswick Acts referring to affidavits to hold to bail ; and a provision in 25 Vic. cap. 31, 1862, that the Commissioners appointed in the United Kingdom, or in the islands Jersey, Guernsey, Alderney, Sark or Man, to take affidavits &c., " shall be persons who have authority to administer oaths in the place where they " reside."

This Act in *New Brunswick* was in amendment of (23 Vic. chap. 26, 1860) " An " Act to authorize the appointment of Commissioners in the United Kingdom and other " parts of H. M's Dominions, and in the United States of America, to take affidavits and " acknowledgements of deeds and other instruments relating to matters in this Province," and was passed at the instance of the Imperial Government, as a qualification of the last named Act. An exactly similar one, passed the year before, having been disallowed as *ultra vires.*

This restriction may have been removed by the subsequent legislation, namely : In 1863 the Canadian Act was passed authorizing the Governor by Commission to " Em- " power such and so many persons as he might think fit to administer oaths, take and " receive affidavits, declarations and affirmations, in the United Kingdom of Great Britain " and Ireland, or any Colony or Dependency thereof without any qualification."

Similar Acts were, in the following year, passed both in *New Brunswick* and *Nova Scotia,* but adding to the above, or " in any foreign state or country."

The *New Brunswick* Act then, follows the Canadian Act, and by section 3, admits " oaths, affirmations, affidavits, or declarations, sworn, affirmed or made out of the Pro- " vince of New Brunswick, before any commissioner authorized by the Lord Chancellor, to " administer oaths in Chancery in England, or before any Notary Public certified under " his hand and Official Seal, or before the Mayor or chief magistrate of any city &c. in " Great Britain or Ireland, or in any colony of Her Majesty, or in any foreign state or " country and certified &c."

The *Nova Scotia* Act is much shorter.

The difference between the three Provinces being, the power of the Government in *New Brunswick* and *Nova Scotia,* to appoint commissioners for these purposes in a foreign country.

In *Ontario,* Not.

BILLS OF SALE AND MORTGAGES OF PERSONAL PROPERTY.

Ontario.	New Brunswick.	Nova Scotia.
Con. Stat. U. C., c. 45–452.	None.	Rev. Stat., c. 119–412.
Stat. of 1865, c. 28—141.		
Stat. of c. 46.		

MORTGAGES AND BILLS OF SALE OF PERSONAL PROPERTY.

In *New Brunswick*, there is no statute on this subject.

In *Ontario* and *Nova Scotia* there are statutes, they are much the same; but in the former the Act more plainly designates the character of sales to which it refers. In both Provinces it is provided that such instrument shall be registered; but in Ontario it is required only when the conveyance is not "accompanied by an immediate delivery, and " an actual and continued change of possession of the goods and chattels, mortgaged or " sold." (Sects. 1 & 4, chap. 45, C. S. U. C. 452.)

In *Nova Scotia*, it is enacted, that " Every bill of sale of personal chattels, made " either absolutely or conditionally, or subject or not subject to any trust whereby the " assignee has power with or without notice, either at the time of its execution or subse-" quently, to take possession," must be registered.

In *Ontario*, if not registered within five days after execution, sale is made absolutely void as against subsequent creditors, mortgagees or purchasers in good faith; but when registered by chap. 46, 1863, such conveyance will take effect from the time of the execution thereof.

In *Nova Scotia*, the time for registration is not limited, but "as against assignees " of the grantor under the Insolvent Debtors' Act, or for the general benefit of his credi-" tors, or as against execution creditors, or Sheriffs &c., levying under process of law, " such Bill of Sale will only take effect, or have priority, from the time of the registry."

The *Nova Scotia Act* therefore does not extend to subsequent mortgagees, purchasers or creditors, who may not be included in the assignment referred to, or have obtained judgment. The presumption of title from possession, consequently operates to the disadvantage of such persons, the sale not being declared void as by the Canadian Act.

In *Nova Scotia*, the word " absolutely" in the first section may be qualified by the 6th which declares :

Section 6th, " The expression, Bills of Sale, shall include bills of sale, assignments, " transfers, declarations of trust without transfer, and other assurance of personal chattels, " and also powers of attorney, authority or licenses to take possession of personal chattels, " as security for any debt; *but shall not include the following documents, that is to say*, assign-" ments for the general benefit of the creditors of the person making or giving the same, " marriage settlements, transfers of assignments of any ship or vessel, or any share thereof, " transfers of goods in the ordinary course of business of any trade or calling, bills of sale " of goods in foreign ports or at sea, bills of lading, warehouse keepers' certificates, war-" rants or orders for the delivery of goods, or any other document used in the ordinary " course of business as proof of the possession or control of goods, or authorising or pur-" porting to authorize either by endorsement or by delivery, the possessor of such document " to transfer or receive goods thereby represented assignments of personal property to " creditors under proceedings for the relief of Insolvent debtors."

Section 7th. " The expression ' Personal Chattels,' shall mean goods, furniture, " fixtures, and other articles capable of complete transfer by delivery, and shall not include " chattel interest in Real Estate, nor shares or interests in the stock, funds or securities " of any Government, or in the capital or property of any incorporated Joint Stock Com-" pany, nor choses in action."

In the Uppper Canada Act, there is also a provision for making good mortgages of goods and chattels *bona fide* given as security for future advances, if the time of repay-ment be not for a longer period than one year from the time of making the agreement, and the mortgage be duly registered &c.

And also that all mortgages &c., registered in pursuance of the Act, shall cease to be valid as against the mortgagors' creditors, subsequent purchasers, or mortgagees in good faith, unless within 30 days after the expiration of one year from the registration a true copy of the mortgage, with a statement of the mortgagee's interest therein, and of the amount due for principal and interest, and of all payments thereon, be again filed &c., with

19

an affidavit of the mortgagee, of the truth of such statements, and that the said mortgage has not been kept on foot for any fraudulent purpose.

The Equity of Redemption on such goods &c., may be seized and sold on execution or warrant, &c., by the Sheriff or officer to whom same may be directed.

These latter provisions are not found in the Nova Scotia Act.

STATUTE OF FRAUDS.

New Brunswick.	Nova Scotia.	Ontario.
1 Vol. Rev. Stat., c. 123–309.	Rev. Stat., c. 118—411.	Con. Stat. U. C., c. 9—30. (Law of England, 1792.)
Stat. of 1860, c. 31.	Rev. Stat., 154, sec. 6.	Do., c. 44—452.
	Stat. of 1865, c. 10 (R.V.) 886.	Do., c. 90—903.

STATUTE OF FRAUDS.

The statute of Frauds in the three Provinces is substantially the same, only that, in *New Brunswick* and *Nova Scotia*, its provisions have been specially re-enacted, whereas in *Ontario* only one or two sections have been particularly re-enacted; the remainder coming under the general terms of the Act introducing the Law of England relating to Property and Civil Rights.

www.ingramcontent.com/pod-product-compliance
Lightning Source LLC
Chambersburg PA
CBHW030554270326
41927CB00007B/914